Medieval Knights

Trevor Cairns

CAMBRIDGE
UNIVERSITY PRESS

Front cover: *A picture from the Maciejowski Bible, made in France about 1250. The artist seems to have been very interested in showing the variety and detail of the knights' arms and armour, so perhaps he has depicted with equal care the fearful carnage of such a fight.*

Title page: *A knight about to give battle. His name is unknown; his effigy lies in the church of Dorchester, Oxfordshire, and was carved in the late thirteenth century.*

Maps by Jeff Edwards
Illustrations by Sharon Pallent

Published by the Press Syndicate of the University of Cambridge
The Pitt Building, Trumpington Street, Cambridge CB2 1RP
40 West 20th Street, New York, NY 10011-4211, USA
10 Stamford Road, Oakleigh, Victoria 3166, Australia

© Cambridge University Press 1992

First published 1992

Printed in Great Britain at the University Press, Cambridge

British Library cataloguing-in-publication data

Cairns, Trevor *1922 –*
  Medieval knights.
  1. Europe. Knights, history
  I. Title
  940.1

Library of Congress cataloging-in-publication data

Cairns, Trevor.
  Medieval knights / Trevor Cairns.
    p.   cm. – (Cambridge introduction to world history)
  Summary: Explores the world of medieval knights, discussing the nature of the ideal knight and how he served God and related to his fellow human beings.
    1. Knights and knighthood – Juvenile literature. 2. Civilization, Medieval – Juvenile literature. [1. Knights and knighthood. 2. Civilization, Medieval.]   I. Title.   II. Series.
  CR4513.C35   1991
  940.1–dc20   90-47627 CIP AC

ISBN 0 521 38953 4

Acknowledgements

The author and publisher would like to thank the following for permission to reproduce copyright material:

Illustrations
Front cover, The Pierpont Morgan Library, New York, M. 638, f. 23v); **title page**, The Centre for Oxfordshire Studies; **8**, Landesmuseum für Vorgeschichte, Halle; **9**, Stiftsbibliothek St Gallen; **17**, Leiden, University Library (Periz. F. 17, f. 22r); **20**, Tapisserie de Bayeux et avec autorisation spéciale de la Ville de Bayeux; **22**, The Pierpont Morgan Library, New York (Stavelot Triptych); **23**, from Wilmot-Buxton: *The Story of the Crusades*, Harrap, 1949; **25**, Archivo Historico Nacional, Madrid; **29**, Lauros–Giraudon; **31**, **32**, Universitätsbibliothek, Heidelberg (Cod. Pal. Germ. 848, Bl. 54r); **33**, Mansell Collection; **34**, by permission of the British Library (Cott. Nero D IX. f. 51); **36**, by permission of the British Library (Ms Roy 19 Ci f. 204v); **38**, The Master and Fellows of Corpus Christi College, Cambridge; **39 1**, by permission of the Syndics of the Cambridge University Library (from *Rothero: Scottish & Welsh Wars*, Osprey, 1984); **39 c**, by courtesy of Cambridge Mediaeval Brass Rubbing Centre; **39 r**, The Pierpont Morgan Library, New York (M. 638, f. 28v); **41**, by permission of the British Library (BL/C/Ms/169; **42**, by permission of the British Library (Ms Royal 14 EII fo. 338); **45**, The Bodleian Library, University of Oxford (Ms Bodley 264, f. 82v); **47**, by permission of the British Library (Ms. Cott. Nero DI f. 3); **49**, **50**, by permission of the British Library (The Luttrell Psalter, Add Ms. 42130 ff); **51**, SCALA/Duomo, Firenze; **52**, by kind permission of St Mary's Church Stoke D'Abernon; **54**, The Metropolitan Museum of Art, The Bashford Dean Memorial Collection, Gift of Helen Fahnestock Hubbard, 1992, in memory of her father Harris C. Fahnestock. (29./54.3); **57**, Bibliothèque Nationale, Paris (Bibliothèque de l'Arsenal, Paris); **59 1**, reproduced by permission of the Trustees of the Wallace Collection; **59 r**, Kunsthistorisches Museum, Vienna; **61**, by permission of the British Library/by permission of the Syndics of the Cambridge University Library (from *Cornish: Henry VIII's Army*, Osprey, 1987); **62**, the Board of Trustees of the Royal Armouries; **63**, by permission of the Syndics of the Cambridge University Library, from *Doré's Illustrations for Don Quixote;* **64**, by permission of the Syndics of the Cambridge University Library.

Extracts
24, *The Autobiography of Ousama*, translated by G. R. Potter, Routledge, London, 1929; **37**, reprinted by permission of Faber and Faber Ltd from *The Flower of Chivalry*, Georges Duby, translated by Richard Howard, London 1986; **44**, *The Unconquered Knight; a chronicle of the deeds of Don Pero Niño, Count of Buelna*, Gutierre Diaz de Gamez, translated and selected by Joan Evans, Routledge, London, 1928.

Contents

1 Warriors and horses

The soldier and the warrior

To understand the beginnings of medieval knights, we must look back beyond the Middle Ages, to the fourth century, the time when the Roman Empire was holding its long northern frontier against the peoples known as the barbarians.

The Roman soldier

The Romans were soldiers, the barbarians were warriors.

The Roman imperial army was professional. The men enlisted for a fixed time, were paid and fed, clothed and housed. They were formed into regular units, from small squads to legions numbering thousands, and were commanded by regular officers. They were trained to march or fight in well-tried formations, almost like a machine. If we allow for the changes in weapons and methods of warfare, the Roman army was the sort of well-organised, highly efficient force of professionals that many modern states employ today.

Behind the protection of the army, the citizens of the Roman Empire lived in peace, the *pax Romana*. Most of them lived by farming, many working on the estates of rich land-owners. The whole Empire was studded with towns and splendid cities and was covered by a marvellous network of roads that carried merchants, officials from the government and, in time of trouble, soldiers. When the Roman Republic was struggling for survival and then greatness, the legions had been filled with only Roman citizens; but under the emperors, from the first century AD onwards, the citizens were increasingly expected to be obedient civilians, paying taxes to support the army rather than taking up arms themselves.

The barbarian warrior

The Germanic barbarians who lived in the forested lands beyond the Roman Empire's northern frontiers, across the Danube and Rhine, had a totally different way of life. They had no cities, no roads, no all-powerful government. They lived in wooden villages, raising their crops and herds and sometimes hunting. There was no equivalent of the *pax Romana* here, as each tribe had to look after itself. People depended on their own kinsfolk and chief for protection and support.

Among the barbarians every grown man was a warrior. When a boy was old and strong enough there would be a ceremony to mark his becoming a full member of the tribe, and the presents he received at this ceremony were weapons. From now on he had to be ready to fight whenever his people went to war. This was his duty and also his right: only free men were allowed to carry arms. To be a free man and a warrior meant the same thing.

There were some men who proved to be such good fighters that chiefs or even kings would admit them as members of their chosen war-band, their 'companions'. They became full-time guards and helpers of their lord, the chief or king. They had to show all the qualities of a true warrior. Of course a warrior had to be strong and skilful with weapons, but these physical advantages were useless without courage. A warrior had to be fearless, wanting to live well but not expecting to live long. Indeed, it was far better to die in battle, sword in hand, than to decay slowly into a weak, miserable old age. Many believed that the souls of those who died bravely in battle were carried up to a warrior's paradise (the Norsemen called it *Valhalla*), where the heroes spent their days in battle and their nights in feasting.

With courage went loyalty. A warrior pledged his life to his lord and would die in battle to protect him. If his lord was killed, he had to avenge him. If the battle was lost he would not flee, but would fight to the last.

In return, the lord had to be loyal to his chosen warriors, and generous. A true lord – and also any warrior who wanted to be admired, as most did – must never be mean. So a great chief or king would feast his companions at his table. In the firelight they would eat and drink, talk of their victories and listen to minstrels singing long poems about famous heroes.

Fame was what the warrior wanted most, more even than the gold rings and richly decorated weapons that his lord might give him. If, by his mighty deeds – and, of course, his generosity – he caused the minstrels to sing his praises, he could feel that he had earned the name of a great warrior, and this was the highest that any man could attain.

A warrior of about AD 500

The warrior wears a mail shirt over a thick woollen or perhaps leather tunic. His helmet has a nasal to protect his face and a mail curtain for the sides and back of head and neck.

For the rest he relies on his circular shield, wood covered with leather, which he grasps by an iron bar fixed across a hole in the middle; the hole is covered by a large iron boss (which can also be used to punch an opponent). The spear is his thrusting weapon, a sharp iron blade on a tough ash shaft, and the long, straight, double-edged sword is meant for great sweeping blows.

Helmets were commonly constructed with a frame of brow-rim and cross-arches riveted together, the spaces between filled by shaped iron plates and the face and neck defences hanging from the rim.

(top) This helmet was found in a Frankish grave at Morken, western Germany, and strongly resembles a late Roman design.

(bottom) This helmet comes from Benty Grange, Derbyshire; though little remains of face and neck guards, there is still a fine boar crest, like those mentioned in the Anglo-Saxon epic of Beowulf.

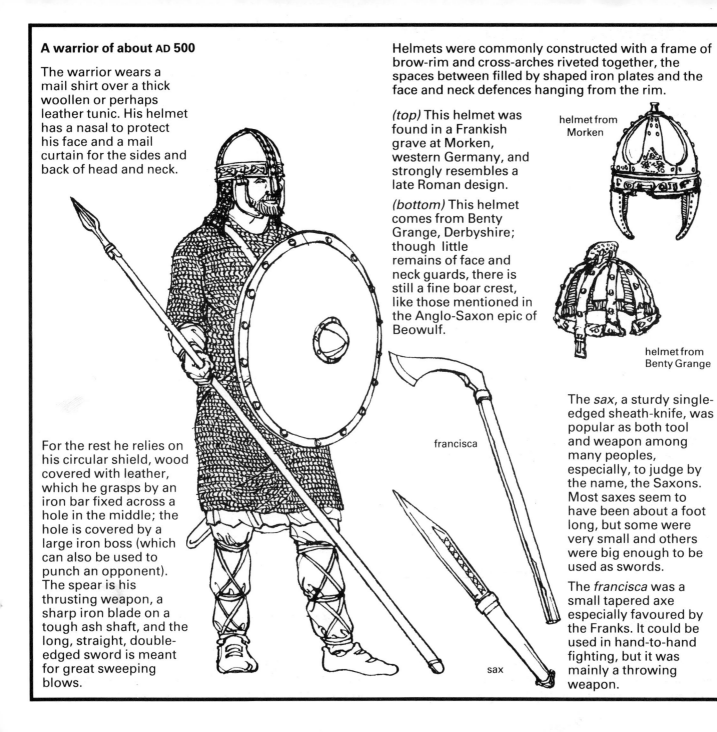

helmet from Morken

helmet from Benty Grange

francisca

sax

The *sax*, a sturdy single-edged sheath-knife, was popular as both tool and weapon among many peoples, especially, to judge by the name, the Saxons. Most saxes seem to have been about a foot long, but some were very small and others were big enough to be used as swords.

The *francisca* was a small tapered axe especially favoured by the Franks. It could be used in hand-to-hand fighting, but it was mainly a throwing weapon.

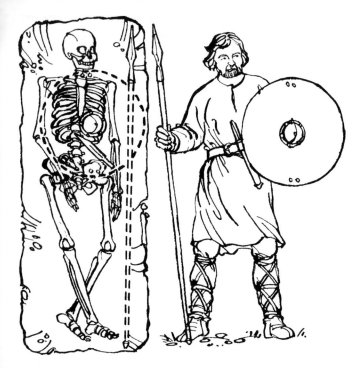

The barbarians settling in Britain were mainly Anglo-Saxons, who formed the first English kingdoms. Excavations in early English cemeteries have revealed that most men were buried with only a spear and shield, and perhaps a knife or axe at the belt; about one in ten had a sword, and there is little sign of mail or metal helmet.

The drawing on the left shows a fairly typical grave at Petersfinger, Wiltshire. On the right is an artist's impression of the peasant warrior when he was alive.

Barbarian kingdoms of the West

An army of tribal warriors would usually stand little chance against an army of well-equipped, disciplined soldiers. For hundreds of years the Roman army had been able to hold or to push forward the frontiers of their Empire. But in the fourth and fifth centuries AD the Empire began to weaken. At the same time the barbarians pressed harder and harder against its frontiers, largely because they themselves were being pushed by other barbarians migrating from the north and east. The Roman defences cracked. Goths, Vandals, Franks, Angles, Saxons and many others forced their way into the Empire's western provinces. They looted and often ruined towns and villages – we still use the word 'vandalism' today – but eventually they tried to settle and establish kingdoms within the Roman Empire. The barbarian leaders did not destroy everything Roman. When they settled in a Roman province they took what land they needed and made themselves rulers, but they often kept former Roman officials in their old jobs, as they were more likely to run districts smoothly, restore prosperity and raise taxes. Some barbarian kings even asked the emperor to recognise their authority by giving them Roman titles.

But in fact it was impossible to repair the machine of Roman government. The *pax Romana* had been finally shattered, and the barbarian kingdoms were constantly fighting among themselves. The new masters remained warriors first and foremost. Trade and towns declined amidst the turmoil, and people had to rely more and more on what they could grow and make in their villages and farms. Even more obviously than before, it was land that brought wealth and power, or at least the means to feed a family.

However, the influence of Rome remained strong. In many areas there remained far more of the Romanised population than there were barbarian settlers or rulers. These settlers soon learnt the local Latin dialect and eventually forgot their native Germanic speech. Modern Italy, Spain, Portugal and France have Romance or Latin-based languages, though all of them were settled by Ostrogoths, Visigoths, Franks, Lombards and others. It was where Roman civilisation had taken less firm root, in the frontier provinces along the Danube and Rhine and in Britain, that German, Dutch and English prevailed.

Christian influences

Of all the new ideas the barbarians accepted from Rome, the most profound was religious. About a century before the great barbarian invasions, the Roman Emperor Constantine I, who reigned from 306 to 337, had made Christianity the official religion of the Empire. Churches and priests had appeared in every town, and had been organised along Roman lines.

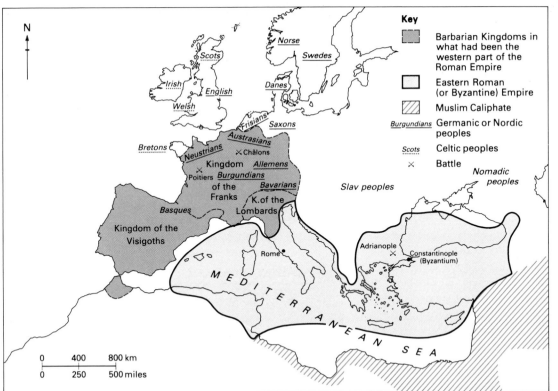

The map includes the following labels: Norse, Scots, Swedes, Irish, English, Danes, Welsh, Frisians, Saxons, Bretons, Austrasians, Neustrians, ×Châlons, Kingdom, Allemens, ×Poitiers, Burgundians, of the Franks, Bavarians, K.of the Lombards, Basques, Kingdom of the Visigoths, Rome, Slav peoples, Nomadic peoples, Adrianople ×, Constantinople (Byzantium), MEDITERRANEAN SEA

Key

- Barbarian Kingdoms in what had been the western part of the Roman Empire
- Eastern Roman (or Byzantine) Empire
- Muslim Caliphate
- *Burgundians* Germanic or Nordic peoples
- *Scots* Celtic peoples
- × Battle

0 400 800 km
0 250 500 miles

Bishops, with their seats in the larger towns, looked after the churches in their provinces, and at the head of them all was the bishop of Rome, the Pope.

When the barbarians invaded, the bishops stayed at their posts and carried on helping the people as before. Many of the barbarians were impressed by this, and as they settled down they too became Christians.

The earliest Christians had preached non-violence. How, then, could either a Roman soldier or a barbarian warrior be a Christian? The Church had thought about this problem and now taught that fighting and killing were sometimes right if used to protect God's people and God's work from attack. So it became quite easy for a Christian warrior to think, when he fought for his king and people, that he was doing right. He could not believe in *Valhalla* any longer, but he could expect the Christian God to aid His warriors and reward them with Paradise, while their enemies went to Hell.

Dukes and counts

The barbarian kings had one particularly serious problem. How could they make sure that all parts of their kingdoms were safe from rebels and foreign invaders? They needed forces which were strong enough to overcome any likely danger and so they chose trustworthy warriors to take charge of different parts of their kingdoms. These officers were given Roman titles such as *dux* and *comes*, which became 'duke' and 'count' in English. The king could replace a duke or count when he wished, but he usually left them to govern their duchies or counties as long as everything was going well.

Each duke or count (dukes were superior to counts) had his own band of warriors, which was large enough to put down small disturbances and enforce his authority. But such a force was not equal to a serious attack from another kingdom. When there was war every free man had to take up his weapons and join the army. In some kingdoms it seems that

7

this applied only to men descended from barbarian families, but in others 'Romans' were also classed as warriors; in any case, the distinction probably soon became blurred. The national army of mostly peasant warriors was led by the king, his dukes and counts, and their companions.

The Byzantine Empire

The map on page 7 shows approximately the barbarian kingdoms that existed in about AD 700. Some barbarian tribes had been scattered or conquered by others, while others, notably the Franks and the Visigoths, controlled large kingdoms. There was still a Roman empire on the map but its capital was now Constantinople. In AD 330 the Emperor Constantine I chose Byzantium as the centre from which to govern the eastern part of his empire and renamed it Constantinople. This Eastern Roman Empire, or Byzantine Empire as it is often called, had beaten back the barbarians who had invaded its provinces. The Emperor commanded a well-trained professional army with educated officers who read, and sometimes wrote, books on military tactics and strategy. They intended to reconquer the western part of the empire, and from time to time they regained parts of Spain, North Africa and Italy. Perhaps it was lucky for the barbarian kings and their warriors that the Eastern Emperor and his soldiers often had to turn their main strength against more dangerous enemies to the east and south.

Franks on horseback

The barbarians of northern Europe fought on foot, which was natural for people who spent their lives in forests and fields. The people who fought on horseback were those who lived on the great plains, the steppes that stretched across eastern Europe and far away into Central Asia. They were nomads who were always in the saddle, looking after their herds and flocks. During their years of wandering, before they pushed into the Roman Empire, some Germanic tribes had reached the steppe-lands and learned horsemanship from the nomads. Thus it was the Goth warriors on horseback who shattered the main Roman army at the battle of Adrianople in 378, killing the Emperor Valens. Then eastern nomads themselves, the

Huns, swept westwards, led by Attila. They spread terror and despair, and no one seemed able to resist their swift and deadly horse-archers. At last, in 450, a combined army of Romans and Germans met Attila's army in a great battle near Châlons and drove it back; and it was the mounted warriors who decided the battle, not those on foot. Yet, while the Visigoths, who overran Spain, and the Lombards, who took northern Italy, fought on horseback, the Franks and Anglo-Saxons still preferred the old tradition of fighting on foot.

As long as the Franks and Anglo-Saxons fought only themselves or neighbouring kingdoms, they could continue to fight on foot. But in the early eighth century the leaders of the Franks set about training their warriors to be horsemen. We cannot be completely certain of their reasons, but it seems very likely that the Arabs made them change.

This mounted warrior is carved on a grave-slab of about 700, found near Magdeburg in central Germany. He carries a heavy-looking spear, his body is completely covered by a shield with a pronounced rim and the scabbard of his straight sword protrudes beneath. He wears no helmet, there is just the hint of protective clothing for the thigh and he rides without stirrups.

The Muslim advance

After the death of Muhammad in 632 his followers burst out of Arabia, determined to spread the faith of Islam to the rest of the world. Fierce fighters, they conquered virtually all of the Middle East and North Africa. These were the most dangerous enemies the Eastern Roman Empire had to face, and in 673–8 and 717–18 they advanced to the walls of Constantinople itself. In the west they crossed the Straits of Gibraltar in 711, and defeated the Visigoths who ruled Spain. Within a few years they were masters of the whole Iberian Peninsula as far north as the Pyrenees. A few years later, they were ready to advance again. In 732 an army of Arabs and Berbers rode north to bring Islam into the land of the Franks.

As they advanced from Poitiers towards Tours the Frankish army met them. The battle, which is known by the name of either city, has been judged by many European historians as one of the decisive battles of history. If the Muslims had won, it is argued, the whole religion and culture of Europe would probably have become Islamic.

At the time, the Christians exulted in a great victory. It seems that the Muslims, perhaps too confident after their earlier successes, made the mistake of charging at the solid mass of heavily-armed Frankish infantry, and were broken. Yet the Frankish leader, Charles Martel ('Martel' means hammer) may have reflected on his luck. The Arab horsemen were fast, and could have worn the Frankish infantry down by endless small attacks. The Franks did have some horsemen, but if they had tried to chase the Arabs they would have been totally outnumbered and destroyed. It was also lucky for the Franks that the Arabs were light cavalry; the shock of a charge by warriors as fully armed as themselves, but on horses, might have defeated even them. Such may have been the thoughts that went through the mind of Charles Martel. We can only guess. But what is certain is that from about this time the leaders of the Franks tried to ensure that more and more of the warriors, when they were summoned to the army, would come on horseback.

Henceforth the Frankish army was to contain two sorts of warrior, foot and horse, but the horsemen were to be by far the more important. They could move faster and hit harder. They were the ones whose charges would decide the battle. Other sorts of warrior still had their value, but for hundreds of years the

The Golden Psalter *of the Abbey of St Gall in Switzerland was written and illuminated in about 880. Medieval illuminators usually copied the buildings and clothes of their own time, even when illustrating biblical scenes, but we cannot always be sure that they bothered to get all the details accurate.*

These knights (probably Franks) wear good coats of mail (or possibly scale), helmets with brims and ridges (none of this type has ever been found) and boots that they thrust into their long stirrups. Shields and swords are mostly hidden on their left, but we see their spears and a ferocious dragon standard, probably stiffened inside.

horsemen were to be acknowledged as the masters of the battlefields of Europe. The earliest medieval knights had arrived.

9

2 The feudal knight

The rise of the early knights

Charles the Great, or Charlemagne, became King of the Franks in 771. When he died in 814 he was emperor of most of western Europe. His empire was meant to be a revived Roman Empire in the West, and was later called the Holy Roman Empire. Charles owed this title to his coronation by the Pope at Rome in 800, but the reality of power lay in his military strength.

Charles was at war every year, often far from his Frankish homelands, and he needed warriors who could afford to spend long months away from their farms. Such men would become very experienced in war, and would be especially valuable if they had the best equipment. In the past, kings had often called up only part of their warrior peasantry, leaving the rest to grow food. It seems that under Charles, while in principle all free men were ready to join the army, in practice there was a regular system for using only a certain proportion of them at any one time.

Wealth, skill and superiority

Besides the obvious need for men to keep the farms and workshops going, there was the problem of the warriors' equipment. Strong iron helmets, mail coats and swords were too costly for most peasants to buy – some had even been known to turn out with nothing but clubs. A small band of well-armed warriors was much more useful than a crowd without armour or good weapons. Charles therefore required only men rich enough to afford full equipment to come to his army. Poorer folk were grouped, according to how much they possessed, in twos or fours or sixes, and each group had to find one complete set of equipment; then one member of the group had to join the army. It was a practical improvement, but it was to have the effect – probably unforeseen – of dividing the people into two classes: those who fought, and those who merely worked

The three main methods of constructing armour in the early Middle Ages

mail

Mail *consisted of iron rings interwoven to form a close-mesh net. Normally each ring was made open, and the two ends were riveted together after it had been slid round its neighbours, but it was also possible to have every other ring made solid from the start. Mail was strong and flexible, but the rings could be burst open.*

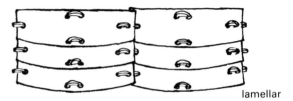

lamellar

Lamellar *armour consisted of small plates (lamellae) tied close together by leather thongs. It presented a firmer, smoother surface than mail, but it was less flexible and the thonging could wear thin, break or be cut.*

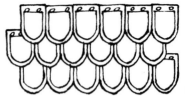

scale

Scale *armour consisted of overlapping rows of scales riveted to a leather garment. It was reasonably flexible – the size of the scales could be varied – and presented a firm, smooth surface against most attacks; but a strong thrust upwards might drive between scales and burst away the rivets.*

and paid. These were people who had inherited the belief that every free man was also a warrior. Could a man who did not bear arms be the equal of one who did?

One of the documents surviving from the time of Charles the Great is an order to a wealthy and powerful landholder, the Abbot of Altaich, to lead his men to the army with food for three months and clothing for six. It says that, 'Every horseman shall have shield, spear, sword, dagger, bow and quiver.' Perhaps it was assumed that helmet and mail coat were the normal dress of a warrior, but it was necessary to be clear about the weapons: they included the bow, which many warriors were unwilling to use in battle. According to the old traditions, a real warrior stood up to his enemy, face to face and sword to sword. A bow was good for hunting or sport, but in battle it should be left to those who lacked the stature – or courage – to give and take hard blows. Why, then, did Charles, himself a mighty warrior of the old tradition, try to insist on bows? It may be that he was thinking of the Avars. These were nomad horse-archers, like the Huns three centuries before, who had plunged into Europe. Charles had finally crushed them, but his men may often have suffered from their arrows, shot from a distance. Whatever his motives, the attempt to introduce bows was a failure. The Frankish horsemen never became horse-archers, nor did the knights who came after them.

The old barbarian spirit was in these Frankish riders. Their vision of battle was to crash straight into the enemy and beat them down by sheer weight, strength and well-aimed blows. But to prepare for even these simple tactics a man needed wealth and time. A horse was expensive, especially one powerful enough to carry a fully armed warrior and brave enough to go unflinching into the noise and pain of battle. A knight must spend a long time training and looking after his warhorse. He needed grooms to help him, and other horses to ride on the march so as not to tire his charger. He had to practise using weapons from the saddle, quite different from wielding a spear and sword on foot. Stirrups were coming into general use by now, and they made it easier to balance in the saddle while wearing mail, carrying a shield, guiding the horse and striking hard blows. But even with stirrups and improved saddles it was only constant practice that made a skilled knight; and an unskilled knight was useless.

No peasant could possibly manage all this. A knight must

The nomad herdsmen of the steppes, Huns, Avars, Magyars, Turks, Mongols and others, had a long tradition of being expert horse-archers. With their short but powerful bows they could shoot rapidly, wounding, crippling and killing men and horses. When attacked, they fled. When their pursuers gave up, they returned with their arrows.

This drawing of a later medieval wall-painting from Qasr al Hayr, Syria, gives a good idea of how they fought and why stronger but slower horsemen found it so difficult to overcome them.

either be wealthy himself, or be the follower of some duke or count as the 'companions' had been, or be supported by groups of peasants such as Charles had organised. But however they found the resources they needed, the mailed horsemen formed an upper class of warriors. Whether born and brought up with these privileges, or selected because they showed the right qualities, they could not doubt their importance. Simply sitting high while the rest walked, being in control of strength and speed far beyond any human's, was enough to make a rider feel superior, and in addition he had the assurance of being one of those who decided the fortune of battles and the fate of kingdoms.

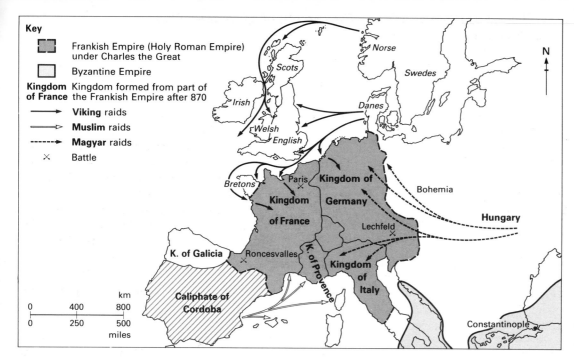

Key

Frankish Empire (Holy Roman Empire) under Charles the Great

Byzantine Empire

Kingdom of France Kingdom formed from part of the Frankish Empire after 870

→ **Viking** raids

⇒ **Muslim** raids

⤏ **Magyar** raids

× Battle

Norse

Scots

Swedes

Irish

Danes

Welsh

English

Bretons

Paris

Kingdom of Germany

Bohemia

Kingdom of France

Hungary

Lechfeld

K. of Galicia

Roncesvalles

K. of Provence

Kingdom of Italy

Caliphate of Cordoba

km
0   400   800
0   250   500
miles

Constantinople

The break-up of Charles the Great's Empire

The Empire in chaos

Civil wars

The Holy Roman Empire was too big for any one man to rule, except the man who built it. His son, Louis the Pious, was well-meaning but not tough enough. He tried to solve the problem of size by appointing his sons sub-kings over different parts of the Empire. The young men were jealous of each other, and there were plenty of ambitious counts and dukes who thought that they could increase their own power by backing one prince against another. The Empire was torn apart in a series of wars between the rivals and their backers. At last, in about 870, two main kingdoms emerged: France in the west and Germany in the east, with the German king keeping the title of Holy Roman Emperor from 911 onwards.

The men who could tip the scales one way or another in these wars were the dukes and counts. They controlled their districts and commanded the warriors there, both their own followers and the freemen who could be summoned to the army. They demanded rewards for their support. Above all, they insisted on something that they had wanted for a long time, but had never been able to force or wheedle out of previous kings: the right to pass on their titles and powers to their sons. Until this time they had been the king's officers, depending on the royal favour and liable to dismissal if they lost it. Now they became the hereditary lords of whole provinces. The kings who allowed hereditary titles weakened themselves and their successors for centuries to come.

The Vikings

Meanwhile, other troubles were pressing upon France and Germany. Men of the Norse lands – Norwegians, Danes and Swedes – had begun to make Viking voyages, ready to trade, rob or conquer wherever they saw an opening. Their first small raids had struck the Empire in the time of Charles the Great, and as the ninth century went on they became bigger and more devastating – no longer a few shiploads of raiders, but fleets and armies. Starting from surprise attacks on unprotected coasts and sailing away before large forces could gather against them, the Vikings became strong and bold enough to sail up rivers, build fortified camps and control whole provinces. The king of France proved quite incapable of organising his dukes and counts to co-operate properly. Each one was more anxious to look after himself than to help others, and would probably not be sorry to see his rivals weakened by the plundering Norsemen.

From the autumn of 885 to the summer of 886 the city of Paris heroically blocked the advance of a Viking army that was trying to sail up the river Seine and attack central France, but then the king himself bribed them to go away and attack Burgundy, where the count had revolted. By the beginning of the tenth century the Norsemen were so firmly the masters of the land around the mouth of the Seine that in 912 the king had to recognise their leader, Rolf the Ganger, as duke when he agreed to become a Christian. The Norsemen's lands became the Duchy of Normandy.

By the time the Viking attacks came to an end in the tenth century, the king of France was left with very little power. The great dukes and counts did as they pleased in their own lands. They obeyed the king only if it suited them and did not hesitate to fight him if he offended them. For the next two centuries the kings of France could hardly be said to rule beyond the region around Paris, where they lived.

The Magyars

In Germany there were Viking attacks too and there was a constant struggle against the Slav tribes to the east. The most damaging attacks, however, came from the Magyars. These were yet another wave of nomad horsemen from the steppes who had wandered westwards and lived on the plains of what is now Hungary. Swarms of them would strike suddenly across the land, robbing and killing. They were so fast on their steppe horses that they could either escape a large army or wear it down by shooting from a distance. For many years the Magyars brought terror to northern Italy, southern and central Germany and even to south-eastern France.

The Germans, more fortunate than the French, had strong kings who first checked the Magyars by building fortified towns, and then caught and destroyed their main forces. But the dukes and counts also built strongholds and employed strong bands of knights to resist the raiders, and so they too became very powerful, as in France.

The growth of a feudal society

Lords and peasants

The dukes and counts were still the subjects of the king. They held their land because he had given it to them, and in return they were supposed to keep it safe and to lead their armed men to the army when the king summoned them. In fact, though, they were the people who really controlled the military power of the kingdom, because they were in direct command of the knights. They were well aware of this, and they had also learnt the value of fortification. If they lived behind earthworks, palisades or walls, on high mounds or in towers, they could hold off sudden attacks from foreign raiders, from greedy neighbours or even from the king. They began to build castles.

While the strong were growing stronger, the ordinary countryfolk, the peasants who made up the great bulk of the population, were much worse off. In times of trouble, war and famine, they were the ones who suffered most. They needed protection, but the days when they could have relied on kinsfolk or chief had passed long ago. They had to look to the nearest man of power – perhaps the duke or count – who had wealth, armed followers and a stronghold. This man would extend his protection at a price. The peasant must accept him as lord and give him his land. The peasant would go on working the land, but pay part of his crop to the lord, do some work on the lord's farms and settle his disputes at the lord's court. Bound to the lord and the land, he was now a serf. This was not a new idea. Something similar had been common in late Roman times and may have survived in places when the barbarians took control. Conditions and details varied from place to place, and it was never a neat, regular system that applied everywhere; but generally in most of western Europe the ordinary people who worked on the land had little power.

This had a great deal to do with their value as warriors. Often a peasant who was a serf was not expected to bear arms, and only free peasants were affected by orders to join the army. Peasants were not much valued in battle because most of them could not afford good weapons and armour, let alone a horse. They were only a crowd of footmen, and not very well armed at that.

The great division in society was between the nobles and the common people. The knights came in between them.

The nobles were the small superior class of kings, dukes, counts and their families, born to fight and rule.

People, nobles and knights

Knights were not of noble birth, but they fought and did not work; the nobles relied on them.

The common people were the vast majority, mostly peasants (both free and unfree), with smaller groups of merchants and craftsmen and women; born to live by working.

The place of the knights

A wide gulf was now opening between the dukes and counts and the ordinary people. It was not simply a matter of wealth and power, but of noble blood. The dukes and counts were the sons and grandsons of dukes and counts. They said they were people of a different quality from those who worked on the land. The knights, though, were neither nobles nor peasants, and they were much too important to disappear into the gulf between the two.

Rather as the nobles had seen that the king depended on them, the knights could see that the nobles depended on them. A count or duke was as powerful as the force of knights he commanded. If he treated them ungenerously, and they began to look for another lord, his power would soon be gone. Knights were not irreplaceable, but good ones were not very easy to attract if a count had a reputation for being mean. A noble knew that, while he must never let those hard fighters think he was soft, he must never forfeit their goodwill.

The noble was not only afraid of losing his armed strength. He had other uses for at least some of his knights. He needed men to carry out orders, to keep an eye on distant villages, and to look after castles when he was not living in them. His most trusted knights were the obvious men for such tasks.

To reward such men it was no longer enough to give them weapons and feasts. Land was the real wealth that everyone wanted. So a duke or count would make a favoured knight the lord of a village, or perhaps more. Just as the count held his lands from the king, the knight would hold his from the count. In return, just as the count was supposed to serve the king loyally, the knight became the man of the count. Kneeling with his hands clasped between the hands of the count, he swore fealty to his lord. He did not have to pay a rent in money, but he did have to fight when called, and if he had a lot of land he would probably have to bring other knights with him. Land that was held by military service, like this, was known in Latin as a *feudum*; later, historians called the relationship of kings, nobles, knights and peasants the *feudal system*. It is a convenient term as long as we remember that nobody then would have understood it, and there could be so many variations and special features in different regions that the word 'system' may seem misleading at times. Nevertheless, the general idea became understood and established in most parts of western Europe.

In its simplest form, the idea can be represented as a pyramid. The king gave land to many nobles, each noble gave land to many knights, and each knight controlled many peasants. At each stage the man above was known as the *lord*, the man below as the *vassal*; a vassal of one man was often lord of another. Anyone who held his land directly from the king, without another lord in between, was a *tenant-in-chief*. Usually this would be a noble, though if the king gave land to one of his own knights, he too would be a tenant-in-chief. Later, by marriage and inheritance, some found themselves vassals of different lords for different lands – but there is no need here to go into the complications that could develop in this supposedly simple system.

Variations: England, Spain, Germany

One of the neatest examples of the feudal system was in England. The reason is that here it did not develop gradually

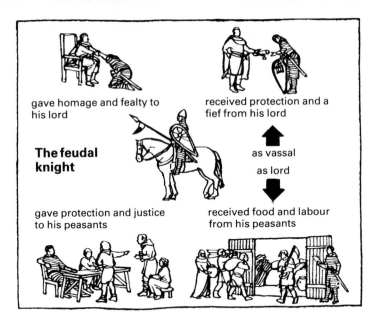

The feudal knight

gave homage and fealty to his lord

received protection and a fief from his lord

as vassal

as lord

gave protection and justice to his peasants

received food and labour from his peasants

as in France or Germany, but was imposed by one strong king. The English, unlike the peoples on the mainland of western Europe, had never taken to fighting on horseback. Their chief men, the earls and thegns, certainly had to fight for the king; they led the local peasants as well as their own men, but there were no knights. When Duke William of Normandy conquered England in 1066 (see page 19) he was able to set up a form of feudalism to suit himself.

He had to set up a feudal system because his nobles and knights expected to be rewarded with the lands of the English nobles. However, William knew how weak the king of a feudal kingdom could be: as Duke of Normandy he had fought often against the King of France and had always won. So he was careful to appoint earls (the English word was retained for what would have been counts in France) only where he thought it was absolutely necessary, in places where attacks were always a real possibility, like the Welsh border. Otherwise he gave each noble scattered lands that could not form a compact power base. The number of knights owned by each noble, or tenant-in-chief, was fixed. It was for the noble to decide whether he needed to keep those knights in his household or to give them manors (as the lordships over peasant communities were called). But William insisted that everyone who held land swore that loyalty to the king was even more sacred than the fealty he had sworn to his immediate lord.

In fact, though, in a society of this sort, built so much upon ability to fight, the king was obeyed only while he was respected as a stern, strong ruler and bold warrior. William took the opportunity of the feasts of Christmas, Easter and Pentecost to gather the nobles (with some of their knights in attendance) to celebrate with him so that he could keep a watchful eye on them, and remind them what sort of ruler he was.

From what happened in England, it might seem that knights either lived in the household of a great noble or were settled on manors. Indeed, there was an expression for the amount of land that could support a knight with his family, horses and arms: it was a *knight's fee* or *fief*. The English knight was seen very much as a countryman, a landholder, and the same was true in most of Europe. But it was not the rule everywhere. In Spain, where the struggle to push back the Moors (Muslims from North Africa) went on for centuries, many knights were townsmen. This was because the king of Castile relied upon well-fortified towns with warlike citizens to guard the frontiers and was willing to offer them privileges, including knighthood for those who could afford horse and arms.

Now there is a sign here that a knight was something more than just a fighting man who could afford the right equipment. A true knight belonged to a superior class with a special rank in society. If a townsman knight ceased to be able to afford the full equipment he ceased to hold the rank of knight; but if a knight by birth became poor he still retained his rank. As a twelfth-century Portuguese document put it, there were some who were knights by nature, *per naturam,* and some who were not.

No doubt it was natural for a family where son had followed father as a knight for several generations to feel that they had a special position in society, far above the peasants. When they became landholders with knight's fees this was confirmed. Yet in Germany the emperor had a class of knights who were not even free men originally. They were serfs, chosen to fight instead of work, and were called *ministeriales*, from the Latin *minister*, servant. Eventually these serf-knights grew so important and wealthy that they became themselves the lords of many vassals and merged into the nobility.

A knight of about AD 1000

The mail shirt, now called a *hauberk*, is rather longer than the warrior's of five centuries earlier, with its skirt divided for riding and its edges stiffened by binding. It has also been extended upwards to form a hood, or *coif*, to cover the head and neck.

The helmet is now a plain cone with a nasal, made of iron plates riveted together without a frame.

The circular shield has been extended downwards to look like a kite; this shape is less handy but it protects the whole left side of a horseman.

Lower arms and legs are still protected by nothing stronger than cloth or leather, it seems, for most knights, though a few important men may have mail. All wear plain prick spurs.

The sword remains a straight, double-edged cutting weapon. The spear may be a little longer, but it is still short enough to be wielded freely.

coif

hauberk

prick spurs

(*top*) This helmet, also made of iron plates riveted together without a frame, was found in Poland. If there was a nasal all trace of it has been rusted away, but the holes round the rim suggest a mail curtain for the back and sides of the head, so the owner presumably did not wear a coif.

helmet from Poland

helmet from Olmütz

(*bottom*) This helmet was found at Olmütz in Moravia, now part of Czechoslovakia. It is plain and practical and has been very skilfully hammered out of one lump of iron.

As shown on the Bayeux Tapestry, the knight's saddle was raised at front and back to support him more securely, it had long stirrups so that his legs were not bent and he could almost stand to deliver blows, and it was held firmly to the horse by broad belts.

The kite-shaped shield could hang conveniently in several positions by its *guige*, a strap passing over the knight's right shoulder. Other straps, called *enarmes*, were fixed in whatever way the knight preferred for him to grasp or fit round his left forearm.

saddle

shield

guige

Knights in battle

In about the year 900 an emperor in Constantinople, Leo VI, 'the Wise', wrote a book of military advice for the Eastern Roman, or Byzantine, army. In this *Tactica* he considered the different types of enemy his soldiers must learn to overcome, first understanding their particular strengths and weaknesses. This is a summary of what he says about the Franks.

> Bold to excess . . . they regard the smallest movement to the rear as a disgrace, and they will fight whenever you offer them battle . . . So formidable is the charge of the Frankish horsemen with broadsword, lance and shield that it is best to decline a pitched battle with them till you have got all the advantages on your side. You should take advantage of their indiscipline and disorder; whether fighting on foot or on horseback, they charge in dense, unwieldy masses which cannot manoeuvre because they have neither organisation nor drill . . . they readily fall into confusion if suddenly attacked in flank and rear – a thing easy to accomplish, as they are utterly careless and neglect the use of pickets [guards] and vedettes [outposts] and the proper surveying of the countryside . . .
>
> Nothing succeeds better against them than a feigned flight, which draws them into an ambush; for they follow hastily and invariably fall into the snare. But perhaps the best tactics of all are to protract the campaign, and lead them into hills and desolate tracts, for they take no care about their supplies, and when their stores run low their vigour melts away . . .
>
> They lack all respect for their commanders – one noble thinks himself as good as another – and they will deliberately disobey orders when they grow discontented. Nor are their chiefs above taking bribes . . .
>
> On the whole, therefore, it is easier and less costly to wear out a Frankish army by skirmishing, protracted operations in desolate districts and the cutting off of its supplies than to attempt to destroy it at a single blow.

These were the opinions of an intelligent, educated soldier on people whom he obviously regarded as being little better than primitive tribesmen. We must also remember that Leo was writing at a time when the Frankish Empire had virtually collapsed amid civil wars and Viking and Magyar raids. His criticisms, though, were sound; knights were still showing the

Knights in battle, as shown in a biblical illustration dating from about 924, also made at St Gall in Switzerland (see page 9). The artist's style is different, but it seems that the equipment of the knights was very similar, except for the helmet. Otto's knights at Lechfeld must have looked like these.

same recklessness and indiscipline 500 years later (see page 55). But when they had a strong leader who could make them obey, their valour and sheer fighting ability won battles that changed the fate of nations.

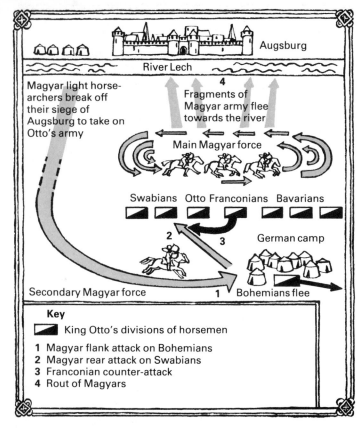

Magyar light horse-archers break off their siege of Augsburg to take on Otto's army

Augsburg

River Lech

4 Fragments of Magyar army flee towards the river

Main Magyar force

Swabians Otto Franconians Bavarians

2

3

German camp

Secondary Magyar force

1 Bohemians flee

Key

King Otto's divisions of horsemen

1 Magyar flank attack on Bohemians
2 Magyar rear attack on Swabians
3 Franconian counter-attack
4 Rout of Magyars

Battle diagram: Lechfeld, 10 August 955

The battle of Lechfeld

Our first example of such a battle is the one that destroyed the Magyar menace at Lechfeld in 955. A huge Magyar army suddenly swept into southern Germany and attacked the city of Augsburg. The city was in grave danger, and King Otto of Germany could not wait to collect forces from all parts of the country. With the knights of southern Germany (Bavaria and Swabia), about a thousand from further north (Franconia, and a few from Saxony and Thuringia) and another thousand Slav allies from Bohemia, he made for the invaders. He took no infantry, for they could not march fast enough. It was an army entirely of knights, organised in eight divisions of about 1,000 each, that Otto led to fight a vastly superior army of

Magyar horse-archers. (Some chronicles put the Magyars at 100,000, but chroniclers frequently lacked reliable statistics, and when they wanted to express great size they simply produced a suitably impressive figure.)

Otto marched so as to come upon the Magyars from the east. They could not retreat to Hungary without fighting him, but it seems that they were very willing to take on his relatively small army. The Magyars broke off their siege of Augsburg and crossed to the east bank of the Lech where Otto was encamped.

Otto left the Bohemians to guard the camp and drew up his seven remaining divisions in line; he kept none in reserve. The Magyars swarmed in front of them, threatening and harassing but never closing. While the main Magyar force was keeping the Germans busy, another force slipped round one flank and took the Bohemians in the camp by surprise. The Bohemians fled, and this victorious Magyar force turned to attack from behind one end of the German line, while the main part of the Magyar army now closed in from the front. The Magyars were carrying out the sort of trap they had used many times before. It seemed that Otto had been tricked and was doomed.

What happened was the exact reverse. Part of the German line was broken but rescued by another division; then all of them charged forward. At last the Magyars were not dodging away but were coming on in their thousands, and this was just what Otto's men wanted. Outnumbered though they were, the heavy mail-clad horsemen smashed into the lighter Magyars, hacking and trampling them down. Confident of victory, we must assume, the Magyars had given battle with a river behind them. Now, as the fragments of their army fled in hopeless rout, they had to try to cross with the knights thundering behind them. Many fell before the knights, many drowned, and many more were slain by the Augsburg garrison as they tried to struggle up the west bank of the Lech. Of those scattered survivors who tried to find a way back to Hungary, many were slaughtered by the country people they had terrorised. After the battle of Lechfeld, the Magyar threat no longer existed.

What does this tell us about the knights? It looks as though they won the battle because of their brute force which broke the cunning enemy trap. But perhaps there is something else. Otto the Great was no headstrong bull, and he knew the methods of the Magyars as well as the fury of his own knights.

Had he tempted the Magyars into closing a trap on him, knowing that this was the sure way of getting them close enough for his knights to catch? We cannot know, but it is worth considering that even if Leo was right about the faults of the knights, a good leader might know just how to use them to shatter the enemy.

The battle of Hastings

Our second example of knights in battle came just over a century later, in 1066, near Hastings on the south coast of England. Duke William of Normandy, claiming the English throne, landed with an army of knights, bowmen and spearmen. The English King Harold was in the north, defeating another invasion from Norway. He led his tired and battered army back south, gathered as many local thegns and peasants as he could in the time, and marched as quickly as possible to face William. Harold drew up his line of battle along a ridge at a place now called Battle, and awaited William's attack; just as William had known that Harold must hurry to meet him or lose support among his people, so Harold knew that William must fight or go back in disgrace to Normandy.

Harold had no knights. Instead he had a picked force, called the *huscarles* (men of the household) mail-clad and well-armed, who fought on foot in the northern way and wielded the great two-hand Viking axe. These formed the centre of his line, with the less experienced and less well-armed *fyrd*, the men called up from the nearest shires, on each side. William placed his knights in the centre and his less formidable warriors on each side. There is some argument about the details of the battle, but the main outline is clear.

William's army charged up the slope, hit the English line and reeled back down the slope. How often this happened is disputed, but what is certain is that his knights – and Norman knights were as good as any in Europe – were beaten back by the armoured axe-men. William faced disaster, but two things saved him. Some of the English, thinking they had won the battle, left their position and chased the fleeing Normans; but as they broke ranks and ran into the valley the Norman knights were able to ride them down, kill many and drive the rest in panic from the field. Against what was left of the English, William used both his archers and his knights, so that when they were not beating back the horsemen they were

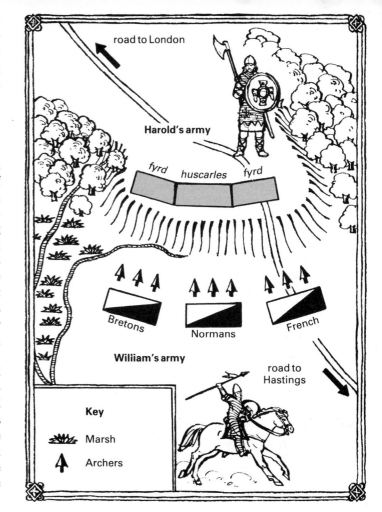

Battle diagram: Hastings, 14 October 1066

being showered with arrows. According to the usually accepted account, Harold himself was hit by an arrow in the eye and, thus disabled, cut down by a knight.

The battle of Hastings made William king of England and has always been seen as a great turning point in English history. Many historians have also claimed it as the final proof that the knight was invincible and that no warrior on foot could match him. Hastings, in fact, proved nothing of the sort, but it suited knights everywhere to believe it.

19

The Bayeux Tapestry

A few years after 1066 the story of Duke William's claim and victory was embroidered in pictures on a long roll of linen, suitable for hanging round the walls of a feudal hall. It is still preserved in Bayeux, Normandy, and called, inaccurately, a tapestry. It is our best evidence of how knights fought in the eleventh century.

(right) *Duke William (on the left) hears a report from a knight named Vital, who points to where the English have been sighted. The Duke is armed as a knight, with the extra protection of mail on his legs and what may be a rectangular reinforcement on his chest. He carries a mace, more convenient than a lance for a general. Vital has slung his shield out of the way and rests his spear over his shoulder.*

(below) *Norman knights advancing, preceded by archers who are trying to weaken the enemy before the charge. Some knights hold their spears as if to thrust, others to throw; it has been suggested that there were two types of spears, and the heavier – the one with a pennon and meant for thrusting – developed into the long lance of later knights. Some figures, like the mail-clad archer, appear to be wearing short mail trousers, but it was easy to tie the split skirt of a mail coat around the thighs and achieve that effect.*

3 The service of God

The Church and the sword

The Church preached peace. Following Christ's example, the earliest Christians believed that they must endure violence without fighting back (see page 7). Those who took up the sword would perish by the sword. Gradually, though, their leaders came to consider that they were living in a violent world, and that sometimes a Christian might have to fight and kill to prevent greater evil from overwhelming his people.

Thus the Church allowed that a government could rightfully use force to maintain justice and order. There could also be just wars, fought to defend innocent people. They also considered it right to fight the Muslims, who declared Christianity to be a false religion, and the Vikings and Magyars who mercilessly sacked churches and abbeys.

Protecting the Church was even more important than saving people's lives, because the Church was the only way by which people could come to the unending happiness of Heaven after their short, distressful life in this world. Human beings were sinful, but the Church showed them how to seek God's forgiveness by trying to make amends. A count or knight who had fought and killed without just cause might repent, do penance, make offerings to the Church and to the poor, and so save his soul from the tortures of Hell.

Good Christians ought to try to serve God in everything they did, and especially to seek God's blessing, through the Church, at the most important steps they took in life. It had been an ancient custom among the barbarians for a young warrior to receive his arms from his father or chief, but by the tenth century a young knight's sword might be placed on the altar during part of the Mass, and prayers said. This prayer was used at Mainz, in about 950:

> Hearken, we beseech Thee, O Lord, to our prayers and deign to bless with the right hand of Thy Majesty this sword with which this Thy servant desires to be girded, that it may be a defence of churches, widows, orphans and all Thy servants against the scourge of the pagans, that it may be the terror and dread of other evildoers and that it may be just in both attack and defence.

That prayer echoes fear of the enemy outside, the Viking, Magyar or Slav. But even in the heart of France, where by this period such threats were usually far away, there was still bloodshed. Counts and their followers continually squabbled and struggled for land and power, and Christians slew Christians. Some of the local bishops tried to reduce the bloodshed but they knew that they could never altogether stop it. What they proposed was the Truce of God, which forbade fighting on Sundays and other holy days; there were a great many holy days, especially if the eve of a feast day were counted as being holy too. During the tenth century the idea spread to other regions, and it may well have saved many lives. Even the most warlike may sometimes have lost some of their fury when they had to pause for a day or two. And they were, by respecting the Truce of God, admitting that the Christian code was more important to them than the old warrior code of their forefathers.

Such truces were never more than local agreements, under the guidance of a local bishop or, in a wider area, a group of bishops. As far as we know, they never had much effect on major conflicts. But during the next century or so the Church grew stronger, better organised, more enthusiastic and more ready to demand the obedience of even the greatest lords and kings. New, strict orders of monks were founded or old ones reformed; they did not lack recruits, nor offerings of land or gold from kings, counts and other rich and powerful men.

At the head of the Church, one Pope after another strove to tighten his control over bishops and abbots, priests and monks – and, through them, over all who lived in western Christendom, from the Holy Roman Emperor himself to the poorest peasant. It was under Pope Urban II, the son of a French knight, that the Church called upon the knights of Christendom to use their swords in the Holy War.

The Crusaders

In 1096 Pope Urban II called a great meeting at Clermont, in central France. Here he described to the dukes, counts and knights the plight of Christians in the east. The Eastern Emperor's army had been shattered by a new Muslim enemy, the Seljuk Turks, and they had taken almost all of Asia Minor from the Christians. Worse still, they held the Holy Land, and made it more dangerous and difficult than ever for Christian pilgrims to go and pray in the places where Christ had lived and died. For centuries the Holy City itself, Jerusalem, had been under Muslim rule, but this new, harsher set of masters of the Holy Places was a signal for action. Rescue the Holy Places, that was the will of God. As the Pope finished his appeal a great shout went up from the lords and knights 'God wills it!' And, tearing into strips any pieces of cloth that came to hand, they pinned them cross-wise to their clothes.

The word spread quickly across France and then the rest of Europe, and thousands of people 'took the Cross' and swore to march east to liberate the Holy Land. They were people of all classes, and the first crusading army to march east was made up almost entirely of peasants and all manner of poor people. Their leaders were a preacher called Peter the Hermit and a knight called Walter the Penniless, but in reality this was no army – it was a long procession of disorderly crowds, begging and robbing their way to Constantinople. When this huge mob assembled there, the Emperor was appalled; this was not the sort of help he had wanted. He was very willing to assist them to sail across the narrow strait to Asia Minor, where the Turks virtually wiped them out.

The First Crusade

The crusade of the knights, usually known as the First Crusade, took longer to organise, was led by great nobles and the relatives of kings, and consisted of real fighting men and their servants. Why did they go? Was it from pure religious devotion?

There was a great mixture of motives among these knights. Some were greedy for land, and hoped to conquer it in Palestine or Syria. Some were greedy for gold, and hoped to loot treasure in the wealthy east and come home rich. Some saw no future at home as things were, perhaps because they were younger sons who could not inherit much, or perhaps they were in debt. There was no lack of knights ready to join in adventurous expeditions, as Duke William had found when he needed warriors to invade England. Some knights may even have been trying to escape from enemies at home or from justice, because the Church granted protection to Crusaders. But whatever other reasons they had, it seems certain that they truly believed that this was a way of earning God's mercy and forgiveness of their sins, and if they were to die fighting in the Holy War they would be rewarded as martyrs in Heaven. (Their forefathers, the barbarian warriors, had hoped to be rewarded in *Valhalla* merely for dying bravely, and their enemies, the Muslims, believed that death in the *jihad*, or Holy War, opened the gates of Paradise.)

When they reached Constantinople, the Emperor thought that these 'Franks' were still much as his predecessor Leo had described them 200 years before: stupid, but very strong. The Crusaders thought the Byzantine soldiers, with their careful plans and clever tactics, cowardly weaklings. Each thought the other treacherous.

The knights charging, with their long lances firmly couched under their arms, are meant to show the victory of the Roman Emperor Constantine under the Christian banner. This is a twelfth-century enamel picture from an altar, and the artist has shown crusading knights of his own time.

It was not non-stop fighting, though. There were long periods of peace when knights with fiefs near the border often became friendly with the leading Saracens (as they called the Muslims) on the other side. Many of these were highly educated and cultured Arabs and the Christian knights often came to admire and copy their politeness and sophistication. Knights newly arriving from the West were scandalised to find knights of the kingdom of Jerusalem who could speak Arabic, visited Saracens, wore long silken robes, trimmed and perfumed their hair and beards and, worst of all, bathed frequently.

To judge from the account written by one of these Saracen neighbours, Ousama ibn Mounkidh, educated Muslims regarded these people from western Christendom as little better than brutes, especially the new arrivals. They thought them ignorant, uncouth, narrow-minded, and sometimes comical in their crudity. However, Ousama also admitted that there were some good men among them, and that it was possible to make friends.

Crusading knights usually despised the Byzantines and fought the Saracens, but probably learned from both to appreciate standards of comfort, cleanliness and good manners that they had not often known in the castles and manor houses of the West.

The monk-knights

In the Crusader kingdom, soon after 1100, a new sort of knight was created. Even before the First Crusade there had been Christian hospitals in Jerusalem, staffed by dedicated men who offered shelter to pilgrims, and looked after the sick and those who had been wounded or robbed on the road. Now these men decided to organise themselves like a group of monks, obeying a strict rule, keeping nothing for themselves but giving everything to their hospital. They were recognised by the Pope in 1113 as the Order of the Hospital of St John of Jerusalem.

Meanwhile another group was formed of men who were more interested in protecting pilgrims by fighting those who might attack them, whether outlaws or Saracen raiders. This handful of knights were given a house near a church known as the Temple of Solomon, and called themselves the Poor Fellow-knights of Christ and the Temple of Solomon, or

Templars. This new order was confirmed by the Pope in 1128.

From the beginning the Templars served God by fighting, and soon this was not only to protect pilgrims but to attack Saracens anywhere. The most famous and respected monk of the period, St Bernard, himself the son of a French knight who had died on crusade, wrote a booklet, *In Praise of the New Knighthood*, in which he said:

> (They) deck themselves not in gold and silver, but with faith within and mail without, to strike terror, not avarice, into the hearts of their enemies.

The idea of an order of knights who had sworn to give up all worldly wealth and pleasure, to obey completely the orders of their superiors and wage unceasing war against the enemies of God attracted many recruits, and many more well-wishers. In every kingdom of western Europe great lords gave lands to the Templars so that they could arm themselves well, hire local light horsemen to scout for them, and build formidable castles. These castles still tower over the landscape of Palestine and Syria today.

The idea spread. The Hospitallers developed into a fighting order by about 1150, though they continued also to look after the poor and ill, as their successors still do. German knights

King Alfonso X of Castile (1252–84) is shown in a contemporary manuscript giving the deeds of the castle of Uclés to the Grand Master of the Order of Santiago.

formed the Teutonic order, which fought partly in the Holy Land but increasingly on the north-east borders of Germany, against the heathen Prussian tribes. In Spain, where the Christians were too busy with their own crusade against the Moors (who still held half of the Peninsula) to help in the Holy Land, the orders of Calatrava, Alcántara and Santiago were founded.

God's foremost champions

The Templars and the Hospitallers became the real backbone of the army of the kingdom of Jerusalem. Their great castles were a shield, and they were always eager to sally forth and attack the Saracens. They earned a reputation for reckless bravery, and if any were taken prisoner by the Muslims they were invariably beheaded because they would never pay ransom. It can be argued that without the monk-knights the kingdom could not have resisted the Saracens. But it can also be argued that they sometimes harmed their own side by plunging into hopeless battles and suffering great losses, and by constantly provoking the Saracens until at last they were bound to attack in overwhelming strength.

These knights developed one great fault: pride. The men who had founded the orders had insisted that they were humble servants of their fellow-Christians; above all they served the poor, and lived themselves in poverty. But meek humility is not natural to warriors flinging themselves into the fury of a charge, and there was also the knowledge that they were the most famed and feared in the Holy Land, God's own knights. There was a saying: 'As proud as a Templar'.

Another accusation against the orders was greed. Though every member gave up his personal wealth when he joined, the order itself became extremely rich. Thus a monk-knight could have the best of everything – horses, mail, weapons. This was sensible, since it helped them to fight. For the same reason they had to eat well, instead of fasting like other monks; there was a well-known joke about a knight who had so starved and weakened himself with holiness that he fell off his horse in battle.

It is difficult to know how many of the charges were no more than envious gossip, and how far some knights had fallen away from the early ideals of humility and poverty as the orders became powerful. But even if they did not always live up to their vows, these knights set an example by promising to devote their strength and skill fully to the service of God. For this was held to be the highest duty of all true knights; John of Salisbury, one of the most famous scholars of the twelfth century, declared that knighthood was a profession established by God to serve Him and bring good to mankind.

The legacies of the Crusades

Saladin and the battle of Hattin

At last one Muslim leader brought together under his rule all the Muslim states that surrounded the Crusaders' lands. His name was Saladin. In 1187 he invaded the kingdom of Jerusalem. The king summoned every possible warrior to meet the danger; he even stripped castles and cities of most of their garrisons. It was midsummer, and Saladin waited behind a waterless hilly waste near Tiberias on the Sea of Galilee. Some wary Crusaders advised the king not to attack, but others called such advice cowardice or treachery.

The Christians advanced under a blazing sun, harassed and delayed by Saladin's horse-archers. The day ended and they had to camp before they could reach water. There was no rest; all night the Saracens shot arrows among them, and set fire to the dry scrub so that the smoke choked the Crusaders' parched throats and hurt their eyes. In the morning they tried to march to the nearest stream. Now the whole Saracen army attacked them. The Crusader infantry, too weary and hopeless to fight any more, crowded on a hill and just waited for the end. One group of knights made a desperate charge through the swarm of Saracens and escaped. Everyone else was captured or killed. This was the battle of Hattin, on 3–4 July 1187, and it destroyed the fighting strength of the Crusader kingdom. Most of the castles and cities had to surrender, and Saladin became master of Jerusalem.

The Crusader kingdom never recovered. The Crusaders clung to a few strongholds on the coast for nearly another century, but none of the later efforts to regain the Holy Places succeeded.

Knights of about 1200

mittens

These two knights, representing Pride being overcome by Humility, are redrawn from a German manuscript of about 1200.

They show the *hauberk* (mail shirt) now covering the arms completely, even to mittens over the hands. Also mail *chausses*, hanging from a belt under the hauberk, now protect the legs and feet. A loose cloth surcoat covers the body armour so that we cannot see if there is extra protection for the chest, but the new style of helm protects face as well as head.

The shield seems rather shorter than the old 'kite' pattern, with the top flattened to allow the knight to see over it better.

Pot helms

The advantage of a flat top on a helmet was that it provided a rim standing out around the head, at just the place where heavy blows were likely to fall. The top two helms are drawn from the seals of important men and show a variety of more or less elaborate designs. The other is a rare example of the real thing, relatively simple but strong. It was found in Pomerania, northern Germany, and may date from about 1250.

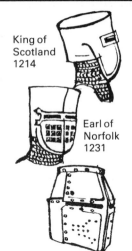

King of Scotland 1214

Earl of Norfolk 1231

Arming the head

The head was armed carefully. First came the padded *arming cap*, which absorbed some of the shock of a blow and stopped the mail from pulling hair and scratching skin. Next the *mail coif* had to fit neatly, so as not to slip, and then its *ventail*, covering most of the face, had to be tied or buckled up. Finally the *helm* went over all.

Sometimes the cap and coif were shaped to fit inside a flat-topped helm, otherwise the lining of the helm must have been made to fit the coif. No doubt there was some form of chin-strap to prevent the helm from being knocked off in battle, but it was still possible for it to be knocked askew. It cannot have been easy to hear when the helm was on.

arming cap

mail coif

ventail

helm

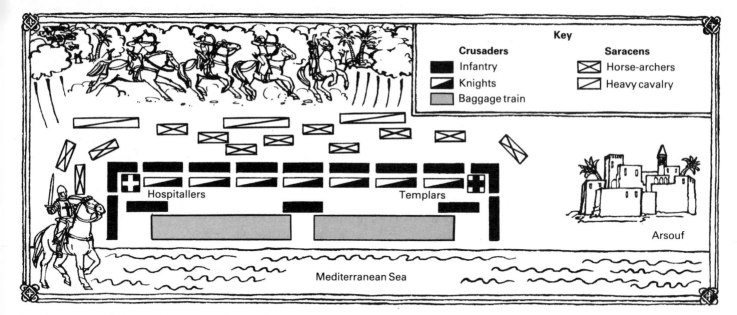

Battle diagram: Arsouf, 7 September 1191

Richard I and the battle of Arsouf

The expedition that came nearest to recapturing Jerusalem was that led by Richard I of England, called Lionheart. It was part of the Third Crusade, which the kings of western Christendom prepared when they heard the terrible news that the Holy City was lost. Richard understood fully one of the great lessons of warfare against the Saracens: that knights alone could not defeat the Saracens, unless they were very lucky indeed. Knights had to be combined with other types of fighter, and the battle of Arsouf on 7 September 1191, shows how Richard managed this.

The Crusaders were marching south along the coast of Palestine and Saladin was very anxious to stop them. He kept on attacking them with his mounted archers, trying to provoke them into stopping and charging; then his faster horsemen could lead them to exhaustion and destruction. But Richard had arranged his army so as to protect his knights and restrain them from charging. Next to the seashore marched the baggage train with an escort of infantry. Inland from them marched the knights. And inland from the knights, between them and the enemy, marched the rest of the crusader infan-

try. It was their job to endure the attacks of the horse-archers.

Richard's infantry could do this much better than knights. The spearmen could stand firm, protected by large shields and presenting a hedge of steel points to the enemy. With them they had crossbowmen. The crossbow was a fairly recent weapon, and when it had first become popular, earlier in the twelfth century, the Church had tried to ban it (except against Saracens and heathens) because of its deadliness.

As long as the Crusaders remained closed up in this formation Saladin could do no more than annoy them a little. Day after day Richard's army moved slowly on. As it approached Arsouf the Saracens grew more desperate to stop it. Their attacks became stronger and bolder, and they swarmed around the rearguard in huge numbers, shooting the unarmoured horses and sometimes hurting the men too, trying to make them stop and charge, and so break the formation of the army. The Hospitallers were holding the rear, and time after time their Grand Master sent appeals to King Richard, begging to be allowed to charge. Each time he got the same reply. There was to be no charge until the king sounded six trumpets, and then all the knights in the army would charge together. Just as the head of the army was reaching Arsouf some of the Hospitallers could bear it no longer. Forcing their way between the infantry, they began to charge. All the while, Saladin's army had been coming closer and closer to Richard's, but Richard had wanted them closer still, so that fewer could get away when he struck. Now he had to give the signal, and all his knights poured through the infantry and charged like a tidal wave. The Saracens scattered and fled, but their losses were terrible.

Lessons and traditions

The battle of Arsouf shows how a first-class general could use knights, and how the experience of crusading warfare could be applied by strong and intelligent leaders. This was an important legacy of the crusades but seems to have been largely forgotten when, back at home, knights found themselves no longer facing the Saracens but only knights like themselves.

The Crusaders lost Acre, their last city in the Holy Land, in 1291, but crusading knights fought on. The Hospitallers founded new headquarters on the island of Rhodes, from which they relentlessly raided the Muslim-held coasts and Muslim ships. In Spain the *cruzada* lasted another two centuries before the last Moors were expelled. On the shores of the Baltic the Teutonic Knights conquered and converted the heathen and ruled until the Reformation. Meanwhile ordinary knights in western Europe still felt the lure of the crusade, and many would spend a year or two helping the orders in Prussia or the Mediterranean.

The last major crusade by western knights was in 1396, and was meant to drive back the Ottoman Turks in the Balkans (see page 54). This was a disaster, mainly because the knights ignored the lessons of past battles. Even after this there were plans for new crusades while the Ottoman Empire grew, but gradually such ideas became little more than pious hopes.

Perhaps the most important legacy of the crusades to the knights was a new view of what knighthood meant. It was no longer enough to be a brave and loyal warrior. Knighthood now meant trying always to fight as a Christian: supporting the Church, protecting the weak, opposing injustice and oppression, extending mercy and generosity and striving constantly to maintain right and put down wrong.

The ideal of Christian knighthood is well expressed in this thirteenth-century carving on the French cathedral of Rheims, where a knight is reverently receiving communion from a priest.

4 The service of ladies

Troubadours and minnesingers

Women had no place on the battlefield. They were not considered strong enough to wear mail and to wield heavy weapons while riding a fierce war-horse. Their role was to bear and rear children, to manage the household and, when their husbands were away, take charge of the whole estate. Marriage was very much a practical arrangement; it had a lot to do with inheritance of land and the linking of families as allies, but little to do with love.

The troubadours

It was about the time when the Crusades were beginning that a new attitude to women emerged in Provence. Here life was not so harsh as it was further north in the kingdom of France. The climate was milder, and the links with ancient Mediterranean and Roman civilisation were stronger and more deeply rooted. The Arab raiders had been less savage than the Vikings and Magyars in the north and east, and by this time the quarrels between local nobles and knights were probably less ferocious. In the castles there was more comfort, leisure and entertainment. The Provençals spoke a dialect of their own, and their talk was not entirely of fighting.

To these households came travelling minstrels with their songs and poems. There was nothing new in bards singing long tales of heroic battles as the warriors ate and drank, but these minstrels brought in other themes. They sang of heroes who performed their mighty deeds for love. These heroes had each chosen a lady whom they thought to be good, wise and beautiful beyond all others, and they would risk any danger to prove themselves worthy of her. The minstrels who brought this new flavour to the songs of the knights were known as *troubadours*, meaning people who 'found' or made up songs. Many of them were excellent poets and musicians, and this may be one reason why the new fashion took such a hold.

There may be another reason why the songs were so popular. In the households of some of the great lords there were many ladies who attended the count's wife. There were also a number of idle knights without enough work to do. The new ideas contained in the songs, which elevated the relationship between knights and ladies to something pure and noble, may have helped to turn flirtations and possibly explosive situations into amusing games.

Perhaps the decisive influence was that of ladies themselves. It happened that about then a number of them wielded considerable power: some were in charge while their husbands went on crusade, and others were great heiresses, holding power in their own right. The most famous woman of her day was Eleanor of Aquitaine (1122–1204) who inherited a great part of south-western France. She married and divorced Louis VII of France and then married Henry II of England, and became the mother of King Richard I and King John. She was a generous friend to troubadours, and so were other great ladies who preferred their households to be entertained with the new poetry rather than with the pranks and brawls of uncouth knights. In their households – or, rather, their courts – a knight who wished for promotion would have to learn to enjoy the songs of the troubadours and to behave as if he were one of the knights in those songs.

The courts of southern France may have been especially good homes for the new poetry, but there were other parts of Europe where prosperity and a taste for a more cultivated way of life were growing, and here the ideas of the troubadours began to find a welcome and to be imitated. There was a great deal of travel in the Middle Ages: merchants going to fairs, churchmen to councils, and students wandering from school to school, for example. Sometimes a great noble or king might hold elaborate festivities, perhaps when his son was to be knighted, and other great lords with their retinues of knights would come from far and wide. At such a gathering every lord wanted to be seen to be magnificent and open-handed. It was a wonderful opportunity for minstrels, and at these festivities troubadours from Provence may have introduced their new style of poetry. In northern France, especially at the rich courts of Champagne and Flanders, *trouvères* (the northern form of troubadour) found generous patrons. From here it was not far to the German courts in the prosperous Rhineland.

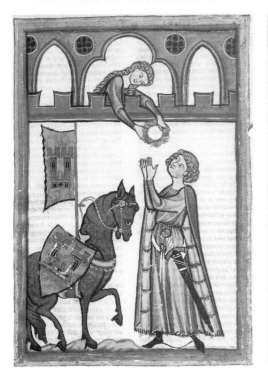

Two pictures of knights with their ladies from an early fourteenth-century German book on minnesingers and their songs.

On the left, a knight is being given a garland of flowers, perhaps as a reward for his poems, by a lady in a castle. Though not in armour, he wears his sword, and his shield and lance are on his horse.

The scene on the right is at a tournament. A lady hands a knight his lance before the joust, while other ladies admire. This is to be a 'friendly' joust, for the lances have, instead of sharp points, coronals with little prongs designed not to go through armour but neither to glance off.

The minnesingers

Like other peoples, the Germans already had love poetry and songs, which were usually quite cheerful and not too serious. At first it seems that some of these poets thought that it was unworthy of a true man to become so servile and soft towards women. Soon, though, the cult of *minne*, exalted and spiritual love, took hold of the German minstrels.

The *minnesingers*, as they were called, were most vigorous at the end of the twelfth century and the early decades of the thirteenth. They introduced a new expression, *frauendienst*, the service of women. It was not simply that a knight should serve his own chosen lady; he should also recognise all women as good and beautiful, while he remained true to the belief that his own lady was the best and fairest of all. A knight who gave himself to *minne*, according to their songs, did not become unmanly and weak; he became better and stronger, avoiding all that was mean and low, striving with greater courage and determination to win victories for the honour of his lady.

Knights as the heroes of epics

Meanwhile other poets were developing the old warrior legends and epic poems in fresh ways.

The Song of Roland

In 778 a Frankish army led by Charles the Great was returning home from Spain, where it had been helping one group of Muslims against another. As the rearguard went through the Pass of Roncesvalles in the Pyrenees the local Basque people, who were Christians, ambushed it, killed all the men and looted the baggage. Among those killed, though not the most important, was the Duke of the Marches of Brittany, Roland.

Three hundred years later the story had changed. Now it was told that Charles had been fighting for the Christians against the Muslims, that Roland was the greatest hero among all the Emperor's knights of the palace (his paladins) and that the rearguard had been betrayed and attacked by an enormous army of Muslims. We can still read this version in *The*

Ulrich von Lichtenstein

was one of the most famous exponents of *frauendienst*, partly because he wrote an account of his exploits.

In 1227 he organised a journey through his native Austria, Italy and Bohemia challenging any knight who wished to joust with him. To every knight who broke three lances with him he would give a gold ring, to any knight who defeated him he would give his horses, but any knight whom he defeated must bow towards all four corners of the world as an acknowledgement of the excellence of Ulrich's lady. As an extra token of his dedication to love, Ulrich wore over his armour a costume representing that of Venus, complete with long golden plaits on his head.

In 1240 he tried to perform another such journey for a different lady. This time he was dressed as King Arthur, with six other knights as part of his 'Round Table'. This time knights who broke lances with them were also admitted as companions of his Round Table. The emperor stopped it, for reasons we do not know. Nor do we know how serious Ulrich was. He spent a lot, thoroughly enjoyed himself, and leaves just a hint or two that he had a strong sense of humour.

This picture of Ulrich von Lichtenstein comes from the same book as the last two pictures, and was made long after his death. It shows him fully armed, with his shield reproduced all over his horse's trappings. His crest, though, is Venus, crowned as Queen of Love, with an arrow in one hand and a flaming torch in the other.

Song of Roland, the first great poem in French literature, which was completed in its present form at about the time of the First Crusade. It is one of a group of epics known as the *chansons de geste*, songs of action, and they are full of violent deeds that pleased a warrior audience. This is verse 98:

> Samson the Duke on the Almanzor runs;
> Through gilded shield and painted flowers he thrusts;
> Naught for defence avails the hauberk tough.
> He splits his heart, his liver and his lung,
> And strikes him dead, weep any or weep none.
> Cries the Archbishop: 'This feat was knightly done!'

Roland himself is shown as utterly brave and honest, as a true knight should be. But the poet also shows him as proud and stupid, unlike his friend Oliver who is just as brave, but prudent. At the fatal battle Roland is too proud to take Oliver's advice and sound his horn to summon aid, until it is too late.

The Poem of the Cid

In Spain the great epic poem was *The Poem of the Cid*, dating from about 1140. The hero was Rodrigo Diaz, lord of Bivar, who had died only in 1099; perhaps that is why the Cid of the poem comes to us as a real human being, not perfect, but still a man of honour, courage and generosity who has earned the devotion of his followers. He is a practical knight who calls his fighting 'earning my bread'. But he addresses his wife and daughters after a victory almost as a troubadour might have sung to his lady: 'I salute you, ladies, and offer you these great spoils . . . Pray God to vouchsafe me a few more years of life, and your honour will be great and men will come to kiss your hands!'

King Arthur and the Knights of the Round Table

But the greatest epic heroes of all were King Arthur and his Knights of the Round Table. Poems about them were begun in the years after 1160 by Chrétien de Troyes, a minstrel in the service of the Countess of Champagne.

Earlier in the century the legends of Arthur had been among those gathered and written down by Geoffrey of Monmouth in his *History of the Kings of Britain*. This proved to be a gold mine for Chrétien and later poets, but it was Chrétien's own genius that picked out the two great themes that were to lie at the heart of all the later Arthurian romances. One theme was how Lancelot, the best of all knights, took as his lady the Queen herself, Guinevere, and how their love brought tragedy to the Round Table. The other theme was how the knights ventured in quest of the Holy Grail, the cup that had once received Christ's blood, and which could only be found by a knight whose heart was perfectly pure.

Running through all these tales was the assumption that in a world where oppression, violence and injustice cast dark shadows over the lives of so many, the knights were charged by God and by their ladies with the task of going forth and righting wrongs.

Courtesy

It is always hard to know how far fashions in poetry, music and stories affect the way people actually behave, or whether they arise because there has already been a change in people's behaviour. But there is no doubt that from about the time of the troubadours a knight was expected to be something more than a good fighter who might be as rough as he pleased. Now a knight had to be acceptable at courts where the influence of great ladies was often supreme. In old French, which was the usual language for descriptions of the qualities of knighthood, *courtoisie* was always placed high.

A courteous knight had to be of good appearance, clean, his hair and beard neatly combed, wearing rich and fashionable clothes. He had to speak well, being quiet and modest normally, but also pleasant and lively. If he could make up poems, sing and play an instrument, so much the better. He must never be offensive and must treat all ladies with particu-

The Round Table, as imagined by a fifteenth-century French artist. Though Arthur presides over the feast as king, all are equal in knighthood and each has his name over or on his seat. Their fellowship was broken at last by two of their own high ideals: for love of God they scattered in quest of the Holy Grail, and for love of a lady, Queen Guinevere, the great Lancelot fought against the king himself.

lar respect. He had to be well enough informed to hold an entertaining conversation, and well mannered at table.

Some knights may have taken seriously the troubadours' idea of what has been termed courtly love, that is, the devotion to one lady who represented all the finest qualities. In theory this made the knight behave better still, for fear of seeming unworthy or of bringing discredit to his lady. There was no need for any physical love between them – though many churchmen warned that in practice courtly love became little better than elegant adultery, which was not part of the ideal of courtesy.

With or without love, *courtoisie* was a new characteristic of knights. There were two others that may have been partly rooted in old warrior attitudes. One was *franchise*, the free, frank and open way in which a knight should bear himself, showing no trace of deceit. The other was *largesse*, a readiness to give, to reward others generously, and to spend without stint on any display that would give pleasure to others and bring fame to himself and his lady. Both of these qualities may have grown from the feeling that concealment, trickery and miserliness were cowardly and mean-spirited. Now they were joined with *courtoisie* as marks of the proper conduct of a true knight.

The knight's return. Little John of Saintré is the hero of a mainly fictional biography written by a French squire in 1455. This shows four stages of his welcome back to court after a successful series of jousts in Spain. First he is greeted at the gate, then he crosses the yard, kneels to receive the king's praise and finally reaches the garden where his lady rewards him with a kiss.

5 The tourney and the herald

Tournaments and jousts

Only a single chronicler records that tournaments were invented by a French knight in about 1060, and that he was killed in one. What is certain is that by the early years of the twelfth century tournaments were very popular among the nobles and knights of northern France and that knights from other lands were joining in. Tournaments, or tourneys as they are sometimes called, were simply mock battles. Since this sort of practice for war has been common in warrior societies from ancient times to the present day, it is not surprising that such games spread among the knights.

In early tournaments a group of nobles with their knights would form themselves into two small armies, agree on a few simple rules and arrange to fight over a particular stretch of country during all or part of a certain day. If some great lord had invited the others, he would probably show his *largesse* by giving prizes to those knights who had been seen to fight most valiantly. Probably much more important to poor and ambitious knights was the general rule that a knight who was taken prisoner must give his horse, arms and armour to his captor and pay ransom, as in real war; a free-for-all raging across what might be miles of country was hard to referee or judge, but there could be no doubt about who had taken whom captive. The knights accepted the near certainty of ending the day bruised and exhausted, a good chance of being injured, and the possibility of being crippled or killed if skill or luck failed them.

Many knights loved it. Some became addicts, like gamblers who cannot give up the excitement that is forcing them into poverty and debt. There are tales of how, after great tournaments, defeated knights would be seen trooping in their dozens to the moneylenders. There are also stories of how knights who had wasted all their wealth on tournaments were saved from total ruin by wives who had secretly saved enough money to rescue them. Other stories, though, are of knights who won fame and fortune through their feats in tournaments. Sometimes such stories were true. William Marshal, who ended his career ruling England as regent for Henry III, first earned a reputation as a champion tourneyer (see below).

People who enjoyed tournaments claimed that they were very useful. How else, in time of peace, could knights practise their battle skills? Tournaments were the best schools of arms. Besides, without them knights would become bored, restless, quarrelsome and feuds and disorder would be more likely to break out.

William Marshal

was born in about 1145, the younger son of an Anglo-Norman knight, and unlikely to inherit lands. He was brought up in the household of a wealthy relative in Normandy, fought in his first tournament in 1167 and won horses and armour. Soon he earned a reputation as a very successful tourneyer and Henry 'the young king', son of Henry II of England and Eleanor or Aquitaine, invited William to join his 'team', where he became the 'star'. He also worked in partnership with another knight so that they could combine to capture opponents and share the ransoms.

This was the start of Marshal's rise to greatness. He had *courtoisie, largesse* and the other qualities that made a knight admired, but he also was clever and shrewd. He eventually became one of the most trusted royal servants and advisers, and was rewarded by being given in marriage a great heiress who brought him the earldom of Pembroke. When he died in 1219 he was regent, ruling the kingdom for the boy king Henry III. He became a Templar shortly before his death.

The mêlée at a tournament was very like a real battle, as this early fourteenth-century illustration shows. It is from a manuscript describing different sorts of sin, which is why there are devils waiting to snatch the souls of any knights killed in the sport.

Many kings thought differently. They saw tournaments as events where nobles and knights were more likely to start or continue feuds than avoid them; where losers accused winners of foul blows and treachery, and where winners ran wild and beat up members of the losing side, perhaps to pay off old scores. Kings of England usually forbade them, except on special occasions when the organisers had to pay for the privilege and be responsible for the good behaviour of their guests.

The Church disapproved even more. In 1130 the Pope declared that any knight who lost his life in such needless fighting with fellow-Christians had no right to be buried in consecrated ground. But knights who were willing to obey the Church in other matters proved remarkably good at finding excuses for going on with tournaments, and there were usually plenty of priests who could think of arguments to allow them to give Christian burial to knights killed in tourneys. It is reported that as many as 80 knights died in one tournament at Neuss, in Germany, in 1241.

Tournaments gradually became less wild and dangerous, not because of Church condemnations but because new fashions prevailed, especially *jousting*. A joust was not a battle but a duel.

Knights had been changing their style of using the spear. Instead of the varied thrusts and strokes that relied mainly on the spearman's arm for effect, knights now used only one style. They held the spear firmly under the armpit, pointed it at the opponent, and charged. The whole weight of horse and rider was now behind the spear-point. Each knight tried to strike the other hard and accurately enough to knock him from his saddle. It demanded considerable skill. Spears had grown into long, heavy lances, difficult to aim on a charging horse, yet it was not unusual for two good knights to hit each other's shields so hard as to break their lances, and both remain in their saddles. Such contests were easier to watch and judge than tournaments, easier to control and much less dangerous. Different forms of jousting eventually developed with their own sets of rules, and larger, stronger helmets and pieces of body armour, too cumbersome for use in war, were introduced to give extra protection.

Jousting probably began in Germany and spread quickly through western Europe. By the late thirteenth century it seems that most tournaments had become mainly a series of jousts. If there was still a mock battle the numbers on each side would be small and it would take place in an enclosure where the spectators and judges could see everything clearly.

Tournaments were also becoming popular spectacles and grand social occasions. In the evenings the knights feasted and danced with the ladies. If they were so favoured, they would carry their ladies' tokens on their armour during the day,

The tournament of Lagny: a minstrel's account

The enthusiasm among knights for tournaments was at its most ardent in northern France in about the 1170s and 1180s. The long poem telling the life story of the renowned knight, William Marshal, written in the 1220s, describes his exploits in many of the sporting battles.

Here are extracts from the account of the great tournament at Lagny. The 'young king' is Henry, son of Henry II of England, whom his father had already crowned, and among whose team of knights William Marshal became the leader.

> Great was the press on the plain.
> Each troop shouts its war cry . . .
> Here one might see knights taken
> and others coming to their rescue.
> On all sides were horses to be seen
> Running and sweating with dread,
> Each man eager to do all he could
> To win, for in such enterprise
> Prowess is quickly seen and shown.
> Then would you have seen the earth shake
> When the young king said: 'Enough,
> Charge, I shall wait no longer.'
> The king charged, but the count
> Stood fast and wisely did not move . . .
> Those then who were about the king
> Thrust forward with such eagerness
> They paid no heed to their king.
> So far forward did they rush
> That they hurled the others back –
> It was no retreat but a rout.
> When they had forced them to a stand
> Among the vines, in the ditches,
> They went then among the vinestocks
> Which were thick and heavy on the ground,
> And there the horses often fell.
> Quickly stripped were those who fell,
> And taken captive . . .

Separated from his team, the king is attacked by an enemy team, all eager to seize such a rich prize.

> And the enemy abounded there
> And seized him by the rein.
> They ran upon him from all sides

> Whereas it so happened that the king
> Had none of all his fighting men
> But his Marshal who followed him
> Closely, for he was in the custom
> Of being at hand, in case of need . . .
> The others were holding in their hands
> The king, each of them striving hard
> To strike off his helmet . . .
> The Marshal then came forward
> and flung himself upon them.
> So hard he struck, before, behind,
> So bravely showed them his mettle
> And so drove and so dragged
> That he managed to tear away
> The headstall of the king's horse
> And with it all the harness, pulling . . .
> But others in the fight strove
> So hard they tore away the king's
> Helmet and sore offended him.
> The struggle lasted a long time
> And was joined mightily the while
> By the Marshal, who fought hard
> And heavily distributed great blows . . .

Yet another enemy team sees its chance to capture the king, but as they ride after him William Marshal charges into them.

> Upon him, as in a battle,
> They flung themselves to the assault
> And he defended himself against them.
> All that he strikes, he strikes down,
> Cracks shields, splits helmets.
> So mightily did William Marshal fight
> That none of those who were there
> Knew what had become of the king.
> Later on, the king was to say,
> And all those who had seen him,
> And those who heard speak of him,
> That never was such a feat seen
> Or heard of from a single knight,
> Finer than the Marshal's on that day.
> The best men praised him mightily.

One knight overthrows another at a tournament in 1233, as drawn a few years later by the English chronicler Matthew Paris.

Many different styles of jousting later evolved, each with its own rules and special armour. There was often a barrier between the contestants to prevent collisions, and the knights displayed finery that would never have seen real war. Nevertheless, it was still dangerous – as late as 1559 King Henry II of France was mortally hurt when the splintered end of a broken lance entered the eye-slit of his helmet.

perhaps a glove or kerchief. As time went on, tournaments and jousts seem to have become more spectacular and less ferocious, though there was always some risk. An element of make-believe or fantasy began to appear in some of the more lavish tournaments. The nobleman giving the tournament might decide, for example, to make it Arthurian; he would pretend to be King Arthur, and his guests would take the parts of some of the Knights of the Round Table.

In the fourteenth century a new variation of the tournament appeared, the *pas d'armes* or 'passage of arms'. Just as King Arthur's knights were supposed to have gone on quests and fought any who barred their way, now knights or groups of knights sometimes set up their tents at a convenient spot and issued a general challenge to any knights who might wish to fight with them. Later, in the fifteenth century, when knights were already losing their value in battle, some of the most talked-of tournaments were arranged in *pas d'armes* style (see page 60).

Coats of arms and family pride

It was important for knights to be recognised in battle. From ancient times soldiers had carried badges, often on their shields, or dressed in a particular way to show the city or legion they belonged to, or what rank they held. Knights at first may have found that it was not difficult to tell friend from foe, either because the enemy looked different anyway, as the Magyars and Saracens did, or because in fights between themselves they could shout their war-cry if in doubt. But it was also useful to carry some sign that friends would spot easily, like the patterns on shields and on the little flags at the tips of their lances (see the Bayeux Tapestry on page 20).

Badges

It seems to have been the tournaments that caused knights to take particular badges and to keep them so that they could always be recognised. It was useful, also, if a knight's family had become well known, for him to use the same badge as his father, or one so similar that anybody could see the connection. Some historians have also suggested that easily recognisable badges were needed as helmets developed and covered more and more of the face, but this does not seem very plausible. There had been hoods and face-guards of one sort or another for a long time, and a painted shield can be recognised from a much greater distance than a face.

A more important change in military costume, in this respect, was the wearing of long sleeveless coats over the armour. The crusaders had learnt from the Saracens that this prevented the metal from becoming unbearably hot in the sun, but the covering was useful in European conditions too. Badges could be painted or embroidered on these surcoats, back and front. In addition, a symbol modelled in some light material, such as stiff leather, could be placed as a crest on the helmet. By the end of the twelfth century, kings, nobles and knights could often be recognised from afar by these crests, shields and coats of arms. They also had the same symbols on the seals with which their clerks guaranteed documents.

A knight of about 1300

From the thirteenth century onwards some of our best sources of information about armour are the life-size figures on tombs; some are full statues, or effigies, others flat pictures engraved on brass.

In the church at Trumpington, near Cambridge, is the fine brass thought to belong to Sir Roger de Trumpington, who died in 1289 *(left)*. His suit of mail is reinforced by solid plates over the knees. The coif is now separate from the hauberk and provides an extra layer across the shoulders. The great helm, here acting as a pillow, has now been extended into a high top, better for deflecting blows and allowing still more space between head and helm. It also comes lower, so that some of its great weight is now borne by the shoulders instead of the neck.

The elaborate sword-belt is cleverly contrived to make the sword hang at the most convenient angle.

The shield is now quite small and much more handy. It displays the Trumpington arms, which also appear on two small oblongs above the knight's shoulders; these are *ailettes*, and were actually worn facing sideways, to protect the neck against sweeping blows. Whether or not there was solid body armour under the surcoat we cannot tell, but this detail *(below)* shows that it was possible. It comes from an effigy [of about 1275] in Pershore Abbey, Worcestershire, and reveals how a 'waistcoat', in this case fastened down the side, could only be seen through the surcoat's armholes.

This picture of a knight drawing his sword comes from a French Bible of about 1250, and shows that already some were wearing a good deal of plate armour on their legs. This knight also wears a 'kettle hat', an open helmet with a protective brim, which was popular for several hundred years with warriors of all classes who found it more vital to see properly than to have the face entirely guarded.

Shield, coat and crest

Meanwhile the tournaments were producing a new profession. As these events became more spectacular, the nobles who hosted them had to do more to organise them. They had to ensure that the right people were where they ought to be and treated with the respect due to their rank, and that the different combats were arranged without confusion. Men with special knowledge were needed, who knew all the important people and could identify their badges at a glance, and who knew the customary rules of fair and foul behaviour in all types of tourney and joust. These men were the heralds.

These experts became more and more useful to the great lords and kings who employed them. They kept records of what happened at the tournaments, of all the knights and their badges. They began to work out rules about the way such devices, as the badges were called, could be arranged on a shield or coat. For example, how a son could wear his father's coat, but with a *label* added to show the difference, and how the second and third sons would have different labels; or how, when there was a marriage between two families, the two coats could be combined in different quarters. And then they naturally kept records of these coats of arms, so that eventually heralds were not only the acknowledged experts on the arms themselves (as the coats and devices came to be called) but on the pedigrees and family connections of everyone who was entitled to arms. Not only were they the great authorities on the art and science of what we still call heraldry, but they were the experts on the rules of knightly behaviour in tournament and war, and they could tell how far back a knight could trace ancestors of knightly class.

As noble and knightly families recognised one another's arms and pedigrees, this could only strengthen their feeling that they were a different breed from the common people. Of course there was also a difference between nobles and knights, but a much less important one; in some places knights were treated as lesser nobles, and everywhere nobles went through the ceremony of being knighted, often with great display and festivity. In England knightly families were not regarded as having noble blood, but they did have gentle blood. They were gentlemen and gentlewomen. They, like the nobles, were supposed to have a special quality, a sense of honour, duty, and responsibility that common people lacked. Families

Heraldry of the Kings of England

Edward III inherited the arms that kings of England had borne since the reign of Richard I: three golden lions (often called leopards) on a red shield.

His mother was a French princess, and the French kings bore a blue shield with golden lilies strewn all over.

When the king of France died without a son, Edward had a claim to the French throne. In 1340, as the Hundred Years War was beginning, he *quartered* the lilies with the leopards.

Edward III's eldest son, nicknamed the Black Prince, bore the same arms, but to distinguish him from his father he had a label added.

In 1405 Henry IV reduced the lilies to three, because the French king had done this on his own arms. Though England had lost the war by the 1450s, the lilies were not removed from the English arms until 1801, during the war with Revolutionary and Napoleonic France.

In later centuries, as different houses inherited the English throne, room on the shield had to be found for the red lion of Scotland and the harp of Ireland (1603) and the white horse of Hanover (1714, separated 1837).

with coats of arms tended to become increasingly a superior caste, and knighthood to be an honour bestowed only on the sons of knights.

Heralds have been called the high priests of knighthood. Adding a touch of mystery to their knowledge of the rules of chivalry, families and coats of arms, the special language of heraldry helped to form an impression that here was something that must be honoured and revered. In war heralds passed unharmed between hostile armies, bearing messages, easily recognised in their bright tabards. They were respected under grand titles, and the senior herald of a kingdom was called a King at Arms.

William Bruges was appointed the first Garter King of Arms in 1415 and wrote a book on the Order of the Garter in about 1430. This picture from the book shows him with St George, patron of England and the Order. Bruges wears a herald's tabard emblazoned with the arms of his master, the King of England.

6 The ideal knight

The hermit and the squire, as pictured in a fifteenth-century copy of Ramon Lull's Book of the Order of Chivalry.

What a knight should be

By the end of the twelfth century the development of the medieval knight was complete. The barbarian warrior had become a horseman and a feudal landholder. His simple code of loyalty and bravery had been extended and refined by the influence of the Church and of ladies, and he had become part of a proud social class whose members met at tourneys and jousts and recognised each other by their coats of arms. Everybody knew, more or less, how a good knight ought to behave, and their ideas were refreshed every time they heard one of the poems about the knights of the past, of Arthur and Charles the Great and the heroes who served them. Still, though, it might have been difficult for anyone to declare confidently, if unexpectedly asked, the full duties of knighthood, or to refer to any authority where they were written down.

The first book about chivalry

One day a young squire was riding through a wood. He had lost his way when he came upon a simple cottage where an old man was living alone. The old man welcomed him, offered food and shelter, and asked where he wanted to go. The squire explained that he was on his way to a ceremony where he and other young men were to be made knights, and the hermit asked him to explain further what a knight was, and what sort of life he had to lead. The squire did his best, but under the old man's questioning he soon found that he did not really understand much about what he was going to become. Then the old man revealed that he himself had been a knight for many years, but when he became too old to ride and fight well he had retired to spend his last years in prayer and contemplation. He told the squire that he must understand the importance of the duties he was about to accept when he was knighted, and there and then gave him a full explanation of what knighthood meant.

That is how *The Book of the Order of Chivalry* begins. The author, Ramon Lull, was born in about 1235, son of one of the knights who had helped the King of Aragon to conquer Majorca from the Muslims and who had been well rewarded with lands near Palma. Young Ramon was the friend of the prince and thoroughly enjoyed all the pleasures that life offered a rich, well-connected knight. It was while he was trying to compose a poem to his latest lady that he suddenly saw a vision of Christ crucified. At first he took no notice, but the vision kept returning and eventually he was convinced that God wished him to give up his life of pleasure and devote himself to trying to convert the Muslims to Christianity. This happened when he was about thirty. For the next fifty years he studied and travelled from country to country, university to university, court to court, learning and teaching, trying to spread his ideas and gain support for his plans to train and lead missionaries to Islam. He wrote many books on religion and philosophy and went to North Africa to try to convert the Muslims himself, only to be shipped back to Europe as a troublemaker. In 1316 he went again to North Africa and his preaching so angered a crowd in Bougie that they stoned him, and he died of his injuries. This was the man who wrote the first treatise on knighthood. It is obvious that the hermit in the book is meant to represent Ramon Lull himself.

He began by describing how knights had first been chosen. Long ago, when people recognised that they had sinful natures and needed to be led and protected by the best among them, they chose one man in every thousand to form the order of knights. (Lull did not invent this idea; it arose from the similarity of two Latin words, *miles*, meaning a soldier and used by medieval writers for a knight, and *mille*, meaning a thousand. It was pure guesswork, and completely wrong, but most people believed it.) These knights were the 'most loyal, most strong, and of most noble courage'. Since their order had been set up by the whole community, their first duty was to the welfare of the whole community. In practice this meant upholding the King and the Church and, above all, maintaining justice for all. To do his work, each knight needed a squire, a horse ('most noble of animals') and land.

The knights would have to fight against attackers from outside and evildoers within, so they must constantly train and keep themselves fit by tournaments, jousting and hunting. But they should be equally important in peace, setting an example of good conduct and ruling justly over those below them. For a king would normally look among the knights for his advisers and ministers and for the governors of towns, castles and districts; these knights must be wise and benevolent. Indeed, all knights belonged to one great order of chivalry, which was quite distinct from joining a particular order like the Templars or Hospitallers, just as all priests belonged to the order of clergy, whether or not they were members of a special order of monks or friars. And just as the order of clergy had been created to lead and govern in spiritual matters, so the order of chivalry was responsible for directing the secular life of this world.

Lull lists the qualities that a knight should display and they are familiar ones: loyalty, hardiness, courtesy, generosity and frankness. He describes how young knights should be trained and suggests that colleges ought to be set up for this purpose (this did not come about), how candidates for knighthood should be examined, and how the knighting ceremony should be conducted.

Lull's book was translated into many languages, including Scots, and when Caxton set up the first English printing press this was one of the books he printed in 1484.

During the two centuries since it had been written other books about chivalry had appeared, perhaps the best-known being *The Book of Chivalry* by Geoffrey de Charny, a French knight who fell at Poitiers in 1356, carrying the royal standard. Charny was a very experienced warrior and there is a more down-to-earth feeling in his book. He is most interested in 'the great business of war', and refers for the most part to men-at-arms in general, whether knighted or not. He speaks of poor men fighting to gain wealth and lands, and others for honour and reputation – but makes it clear that honour and reputation have practical advantages too. Yet he agrees with Lull that the order of chivalry is like a religious order. Those men-at-arms who trust in their own strength, not in God, will fail, but the true knight will enjoy honour in this world and Heaven in the next.

The way to become a knight

A boy of noble or gentle birth – that is, belonging to the feudal upper classes – learned the behaviour and manners expected of knights from his earliest years. In his father's castle he was taught by the ladies to be polite and pleasant, clean and willing to perform small services for his elders. In the later Middle Ages it became quite usual for such boys to be taught to read and write, perhaps by the castle chaplain. Above all, he started to learn from his father's squires and grooms how to ride and play games that would eventually make him strong and skilful with weapons; hunting and hawking were thought to be good training.

Only the first stages of his education were at home. As soon as he was considered old enough, perhaps at about the age of ten, he was sent away to be brought up in another household. If possible, it would be a great household, perhaps that of his father's lord, so that he would become used to living with many more people and amid greater wealth and power. He might impress influential people, make useful friends, look

Don Pero Niño, the Unconquered Knight

In the 1430s his standard-bearer, Gutierre Diaz de Gamez, wrote an account of the deeds of Don Pero Niño, the Castilian nobleman, whom he had served loyally since they were both young men. This is how Gutierre describes the master whom he believes to be a perfect knight:

This knight was fair to see, of a heavy build, neither very tall nor yet short, and well-formed; he had wide shoulders, a deep chest, hips high on his body, thighs thick and strong, arms long and well made, thick buttocks, a hard fist, and well-turned leg and a slim delicate waist. He had a low and pleasant voice and lively and gracious speech. He ever dressed well, with care and thought, making the most of what he wore. A poor man's dress would look better on him than the richest robes on many other men. He had a better understanding of new fashions than any tailor or robe-maker, so that the finely dressed always took him as their pattern.

In point of armour he had much knowledge and understanding; he himself used to show the armourers the fairest shapes and tell them how they might make armour lighter without loss of strength. He was more learned than any in the matters of swords and daggers and bettered them much.

As for saddles, no man of his time understood them so well. He had them planed down and strengthened and at the same time had the wood made thin and the trimmings and straps less. It was in his household that the divided girth, such as they use today, was first used. Of caparisons for jousting he had more than any man in all Castille. He knew all about horses; he sought for them, tended them and made much of them. In his time had no man in Castille so many good mounts; he rode them and trained them to his liking, some for war, some for parade and others for jousting. Hard did he strike with his sword and strong and signal blows did he make with its point; never did he meet a man who cut and thrust so well as he.

He excelled in all other exercises which asked for boldness and nimbleness, in sports of lance-thrusting and dart-throwing. He was a mighty player at bowls and with the disc, as well as at hurling stones. He was also a mighty player with a spar and threw it better than other men; in all these sports he was rarely surpassed by those who tried their strength with him.

Doubtless from time to time there have been men who did one or other of these things in especial as well as he, this one thing, and that another, but a man who did so well in them all generally, a man's body in which all these qualities were united, who accomplished all in such perfection, was not found in Castille in his time. Moreover he used to bend the strongest crossbows from the girdle and drew as straight an arrow with the arbalest as with the bow and never missed his aim. To see him shoot at a target with little quarrels was a delight; moreover, it was no marvel that this knight so far excelled the rest in all such exercises, for, besides the strong body and great force wherewith God had endowed him, all his care and all his means were devoted to naught but to the calling of arms, the art of chivalry and every noble labour.

God had been generous in giving him those virtues of the soul that he divides among men. He was most courteous and of gracious speech; firm with the strong, gentle with the weak, gracious to all, prudent in question and reply, an upright judge and wont to pardon freely. Gladly would he undertake to speak for the poor, and to defend those who commended themselves to his care, and he would help them from his purse. Never did man or woman who asked an alms of him go away empty-handed. He was true and staunch; never did he break his word when he had pledged it. He was always faithful to the King; never did he make treaty or league with any man to the King's disservice, whether within or without the realm. Ever did he labour to defend his King's cause; always did he hate and combat those who rebelled against his King. He was firm and steadfast in all his deeds: never did he let himself be bought by gifts or promises. He was ever liberal and never prodigal; never miserly and never grasping when he should be giving. Never did he give himself up to idleness and never did he waste time that might be spent in the honourable advancement of his affairs. Temperance gave him his rule of life; he was not known to have any mistresses in his youth, and likewise never was he found eating and drinking except at the fitting hours, for he knew the old proverb that says: 'Idleness, good fare, and honour never dwell in the same house.'

after himself sooner and harder than at home. He would be trained by strangers who had no reason either to favour or to expect too much of him, as his own family might. Thus he began his service as a page.

From page to squire

As a page he learned to serve others carefully, gracefully and willingly. One of his most obvious accomplishments was to wait upon his elders at table and to carve the meat for them. Not only must he cheerfully fetch and carry for ladies, but he also had to be ready to entertain them with music and verse, or to play chess and backgammon. He was allowed to take more and more part in the hunt and in flying falcons as he became stronger and more skilled, and he also began to practise the skills of war. He learned to wear armour and use weapons without tiring, to ride powerful horses and to wield the lance, sword and mace from the saddle. On foot he also learned to use two-handed weapons like the pole-axe. But he still served, learning to dress his master properly in his armour, to look after his weapons and to care for his horse. As he passed through his early teens the page gradually became a strong young man, fit to play a part in joust, or tournament, or even in battle. When he reached this level of ability he ceased to be a page and was classed as an esquire, or squire.

From squire to knight

Now the young man's education was complete. An esquire, if he could afford it, would be armed and mounted and would fight like a knight. What he lacked was experience, and this he learned as the assistant to a knight, still helping him with armour and horse but also fighting beside him and trying to defend him from injury or capture. A squire was not supposed to be qualified to take command of a company of soldiers, though in practice many of the more experienced squires did.

There was no fixed time or qualification before a squire could be made a knight. It seems to have been possible for any knight to dub an esquire to the order of knighthood. Usually there was some ceremony, depending much on the rank and wealth of the people taking part. We have to remember that it was the most splendid occasions that the chroniclers wrote about, not the average.

The first detailed account of such a ceremony is from 1128, when Geoffrey of Anjou was dubbed by King Henry I of England before marrying the king's daughter Matilda. He had a ritual bath, was dressed in a cloth-of-gold tunic and purple cloak, gold spurs were buckled to his feet, a shield painted with lions was placed on his arm and a sword hung around his waist. Thirty of his companions – perhaps they had been pages or squires in his family's castles – were knighted with him and presented with arms and horses.

All through the Middle Ages the knighting of princes and the sons of great nobles was just as lavish, often with tournaments and jousts, and feasts for the local people as well as the noble guests. It is easy to see why one of the three feudal aids, when vassals were obliged to make generous donations to the lord, was for the knighting of his eldest son. (The other two were for the marriage of his eldest daughter and for his own ransom if he were taken prisoner.) The knighting ceremony had to be a joyously memorable occasion because it proclaimed that this was the young man who was to take over from

Boys learning to joust with a wooden horse on wheels. It seems that the rider has a choice of two targets; the nearest is simply a painted board, but the second is a quintain, *a device which would turn and swing its arms when hit, and smack an unskilful jouster. The drawing is from a fourteenth-century romance.*

The ritual of knighting

A French poem called the Ordene de Chevalerie (Order of Knighthood), written before 1250, explains in story form what all the parts of a knighting ceremony meant. The story is that Count Hugh of Tiberias, a famous Crusader, has been captured by the Saracens. Their leader, the great Saladin, so admires the knights he battles against that he wishes to be knighted himself. He asks Hugh to knight him, promising in exchange freedom without ransom. Hugh agrees.

1 After dressing Saladin's hair and beard, Hugh prepares for him the bath of courtesy and bounty, explaining that the new knight emerges clean, as the baptised child emerges without stain of sin.

2 Saladin is then taken to rest in a fine bed, which represents the ease and comfort that a knight will enjoy in Heaven, if he earns it by being true.

3 On rising, the new knight is dressed in:
- a white robe to emphasise his cleanliness;
- a scarlet cloak to represent his blood, which he is ready to shed for God and the Church;
- brown stockings, the colour of the earth to which all must come at last, a reminder to be ready always to die well.

4 Next Saladin is equipped with:
- a white belt, to symbolise purity;
- golden spurs, a sign that he will be swift as a spurred horse to obey God's commands;
- and finally the sword, its two edges a pair like justice and loyalty, ready to defend the oppressed.

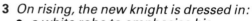

5 Now fully prepared, the new knight should be struck by the knight conducting the ceremony. As Hugh regards Saladin as his master for the time being, it would be against his own duty as a knight to give such a blow. So he goes on to tell Saladin the four things that a Christian knight must always keep in mind:
- never consent to treason or false judgement;
- honour all women and help them in their need;
- hear Mass every day, if possible;
- fast on Fridays, in remembrance of the sufferings of Christ.

his father. And all the other squires dubbed at the same time were supposed to feel a special bond of loyalty to the prince and to one another.

The ceremonies varied a little, but were usually very similar. After the bath the candidate for knighthood often spent all night watching over his arms and praying in the chapel. There was always blessing by a priest. The actual moment of the knighting was marked by a light blow, with the hand or the flat of a weapon. Nobody is sure how this custom began or what it meant. It seems to have been used mainly in France and England before the fourteenth century. According to a prayer book of 1295, the words to be said as the blow was delivered were: 'Awake from evil dreams and keep watch, faithful in Christ and praiseworthy in fame.' In an earlier poem, *The Order of Chivalry*, the words are: 'Remember Him who has made thee knight and ordained thee.' Some have suggested that it is linked to an old custom of hitting witnesses at legal transactions to help them fix the event in their memories, or it may have been a symbol of the hardships a knight must be prepared to endure. Whatever it meant, this ceremonial blow became the main feature of even the simplest dubbing.

Ceremonial had its place in peacetime, but in war men were made knights more simply. Before a battle a group of squires would sometimes be dubbed and then placed where they could enhance their reputation by hard fighting. There were also knightings after battles, for squires who had performed great feats of arms, and they were probably given land as well. The most famous story of knighting comes from Crécy in 1346. Edward III's son, the Black Prince, who had been knighted only at the start of the campaign, seemed to be in difficulties and the king's companions suggested sending reinforcements; but the king said, 'Let the boy win his spurs', sent little help, and the prince earned much praise from the victory.

A squire would feel it a greater honour if he were knighted by a great man, especially the king himself. It was quite normal to be knighted by your feudal lord, in whose house you might have been a page; this also helped to strengthen the loyalty between lord and vassal. But some squires, especially if they were trying to become famous in war, would be happiest if they could be knighted by a knight who was already famed for valiant deeds. As a German poet said: 'The worth of the worthy makes me worthy.' Some did not ask to be

Making a knight, as shown in a thirteenth-century manuscript. The king completes the girding on of the sword and at the same time warns the new knight of his duties. Meanwhile attendants fasten on the spurs.

knighted until they had already earned fame; Don Pero Niño did not seek knighthood from his king until he was twenty-eight, and he had been fighting successfully since the age of fifteen.

Everybody agreed with the high ideals of knighthood set forth in the romances of King Arthur and the treatises of Lull and Charny. At least, that was the theory. But in practice it seems that there were many who did not value knighthood so very much. As time went on, it became quite common for gentlemen of knightly family and wealth to avoid being knighted, if they could. Meanwhile, war remained brutal; while knights may often have treated enemy knights with honour and courtesy, ordinary people could expect devastation and slaughter.

7　The English knights

Knights in the shires

The noble ideals, the solemn ceremonies and the brilliant show of heraldry and tournament can sometimes blind us to the practical business of being a knight. Knights owed their superior position to the crudest of all practical arguments – brute force. Their power in arms was what gave them power in the daily life of the country, through their lands, the 'knight's fees' that their lords gave them. It is true that many villages remained directly under the control of great nobles or abbeys, being managed for their lords by stewards and bailiffs, but commonly the lord of the manor in a village would be a knight who held it from a great lord. The knight would be master of his village or villages, collecting rents and services from the peasants, keeping them in order and settling their disputes in his manor court. At a time when the vast majority of people lived off the land, the men who ruled the villages were the backbone of society.

Both their lords and the king relied upon them. Like any feudal vassal, a knight must be loyal to his lord and follow him to war. In some kingdoms foreign attacks and quarrels between nobles made fighting very frequent, but England suffered less than most. This was partly because of her island position, and partly because after the Conquest the Norman kings kept a firm grip.

In every shire the king's officer, the *shire-reeve* or sheriff, tried to ensure that the law was respected. Every few months the sheriff would hold the shire court, where cases would be judged and where he could make announcements and discuss local matters. All men of wealth and power, particularly lords of manors, were expected to attend. So in every shire the knights, regularly meeting and giving their views on public business, came naturally to think of themselves as the important families, the ruling class. It was also natural that when the king decided to appoint other local officials, such as Justices of the Peace, he would pick members of this class. Thus, as time

went on, many knights came to see themselves more as local dignitaries than warriors, concerned more with the business and welfare of their manors and shires than with chivalry.

As they settled deeper into life on the manor, many knights must have had mixed feelings when called to the army, or when it was their turn to do castle-guard at a nearby royal stronghold. It was a nuisance, but they held their land only by military service. Even if they did not bother to be knighted, they still owed service as knights.

Kings, barons and knights in Parliament

Though quiet compared with many other kingdoms, England still saw some fighting. Sometimes this arose from disputes between the king and groups of his great nobles, or barons. Whilst a king thought he was trying to use, and even increase, his strength to enforce the law and bring justice to all his people, some of his nobles might think he was acting like a tyrant and destroying their liberties. Once king and barons distrusted each other, suspicion could easily flare into open defiance and violence among men who had been taught since childhood to behave as warriors.

The most famous of these struggles between king and barons were in the thirteenth century: at the beginning of the century, when King John offended both the Church and a large number of his barons; and in the middle, when Simon de Montfort, Earl of Leicester, led a party of barons to fight against the misgovernment, as they saw it, of the people who were advising the weak King Henry III.

What was a knight to do if his lord was on one side and his king on another? Probably most knights felt that they had to be loyal to the lord they knew, in whose household they had, perhaps, been brought up, and who was in a far better position to help or harm them than a distant king.

Both sides in these struggles were anxious to get as many fighting men on their side as possible, and knights were therefore vital. The main towns, or boroughs, were important too, because the growing wealth of their merchants could help to hire mercenary soldiers from such places as Flanders. Sometimes the townspeople could also be useful in defending their walls, or as infantry in a battle. It is not surprising, therefore, since they needed all the help they could muster, that rebel

Sir Geoffrey Luttrell

Sir Geoffrey Luttrell, 1276–1345, of Lincolnshire, was a prosperous knight with lands in several places. In the 1330s he ordered a magnificent prayer book; this is now famous as the Luttrell Psalter.

The top picture shows him ready for battle or tourney, with his wife and daughter-in-law handing him helm and shield. We know from other records too that he did his share of military service.

To judge from the pictures in his Psalter, he also took great pleasure in the everyday life of his manors. In lively detail his artist depicts the whole round of the country year – from ploughing and sowing to harvesting and milling.

It all led to the kitchen, where the cooks prepared the food. We then see it carved and served. Sir Geoffrey is shown here presiding at the dinner table, with his wife, two sons and one daughter-in-law, and two guests, Dominican friars.

barons took care to show that they were not only looking after themselves. When they forced King John to grant the Great Charter of Liberties in 1215, the Magna Carta, knights and burgesses were among the 'free men' whose rights were guaranteed. It was even more striking in 1265 when Simon de Montfort, after capturing the king, summoned a Parliament, as the Great Council of England was beginning to be called. As well as the nobles who were usually summoned, he sent for two knights from every shire and two burgesses from every borough to represent the important classes.

De Montfort was defeated and killed soon afterwards by the king's son, Edward, but his idea was not forgotten. Edward became the great King Edward I, and he came to agree that such important classes of men as these ought to be represented. By the time his reign ended in 1307 it was recognised that, while each nobleman came to Parliament in his own right, two knights should come to speak for all the landed gentry of each county, and two burgesses similarly for each wealthy town. The great barons met in one place, the knights and burgesses in another; these became the House of Lords and the House of Commons. Both Houses could offer the king advice and vote on any extra money he wanted to raise by taxation. Thus the English country knights, as a class, played a part in the government of the kingdom.

It was still only a minor part. The lords remained by far the most important people in England, and the House of Commons naturally followed the lead of the House of Lords. Within the Commons, however, the knights of the shires led, the burgesses followed. Though less than nobles, the knights were gentlemen; and merchants, no matter how rich some of them had become, were not.

New knights for new ways of war

Paying for mercenaries

The knights were not the only ones who had been finding their spells of military service a nuisance. Very often the king felt much the same. It was awkward to raise armies of knights who owed only forty days' service a year, and many of them were not particularly skilful warriors. Sometimes it was better to ask them for *scutage*, money instead of service, and then to hire mercenaries. These hired soldiers might not be as brave as the best knights, but they were experienced, tough, and obedient as long as they got their pay. Knights and their lords were sometimes glad to pay scutage, but by the time of King John they were worried about the danger of this practice. They began to fear that the king would keep a permanent army of foreign mercenaries and use them to hold his subjects down. This was one of the reasons for their revolt against John.

Some knights serve longer

It was in Edward I's reign that a new system seems to have been worked out that satisfied everyone. Edward involved himself in wars that were not just a series of sieges and battles against other kings or great nobles, but were attempts to occupy and control hostile countries where the people would take every opportunity to drive him out. In North Wales and later in Scotland Edward I needed men who would be prepared to go on fighting and guarding for months and years, not knights who would want to go home after a few weeks. The solution was to ask for only a small number of all the knights he was entitled to call up, and to take money from the rest. This meant that lords, sheriffs and the knights themselves in any district could agree that the knights who were most willing to go to war could do so, and stay on, supported by the money of the rest. Of course the king still had the right to summon large numbers of knights if he needed them for a decisive battle, but usually it was better to have a smaller but more experienced army.

Peasants with longbows

Of course armies did not consist entirely of knights on horseback. In both Wales and Scotland the English knights learnt again how useful – or dangerous – good infantry could be. The main strength of the Scots under Wallace and Bruce was their spearmen; standing in solid masses, bristling with long, deadly steel points, they could beat off the most earth-shaking charges of the proudest knights. To break these *schiltrons*, as the Scots called their formations, Edward needed the bowmen of South Wales, who had already helped him in North Wales. They carried bows as tall as themselves and shot arrows a yard long. They shot fast, accurately and hard, and their arrows could penetrate mail and even the weaker parts of plate armour. This weapon was the longbow, and when the English peasantry took it up it became the national weapon of England, the great battle-winner of the Hundred Years War against France that went on, with intervals, from 1337 to 1453.

Captains, companies and contracts

The English kings, nobles and knights were not too proud to encourage and rely upon the bowmen. As the war in France went on and on, some of the English knights not only commanded companies of archers in battle, but became their full-time employers. Knights would sign contracts with the king to bring to the army an agreed number of soldiers, some mounted men-at-arms perhaps, but mainly archers, for an agreed sum. The knight would then lead and pay his company, try to enforce discipline and at the same time earn their loyalty by victory and loot.

Also in the Luttrell Psalter *is this picture of a group of peasants practising with their longbows. Tenants and followers of English knights, these were to be among the new masters of the battlefield.*

John Hawkwood

is said to have been the son of an Essex tanner who left his apprenticeship in London to join the Black Prince's army in France, where he became such an able soldier that he commanded a company and was knighted.

In 1360 the Peace of Bretigny ended his employment in France, so he led his company to Italy, where the endless disputes between the city-states offered a rich livelihood to *condottieri*, captains of mercenaries. Hawkwood and his men were known as the White Company, apparently from their plain armour. They soon became known also as ruthless and successful fighters, and were employed by some of the most important states.

Hawkwood married an illegitimate daughter of the ruler of Milan, and represented the King of England on embassies to some Italian states. As long as he was paid, he served his masters well, and eventually settled into the post of Captain-General of all the forces of Florence. Here he died in 1394, and the city gave him a state funeral in the cathedral.

This monument to John Hawkwood was placed on the wall of the cathedral of Florence in 1436, and was the work of Paolo Uccello, one of the leading artists of the Italian Renaissance.

Such knights were not feudal cavalry, but paid captains. Some, indeed, turned into mercenaries; at times of truce, rather than disband their companies, they might go off to seek other employers.

In English armies, then, when Edward III and the Black Prince were winning their victories in the middle of the fourteenth century, the knights were no longer a mass of mailed horsemen, bound by feudal loyalty, whose shattering charge would decide the battle. And in the English countryside, men classed as knights were quite likely to stay on their manors and leave the war in France to those knights who wanted to seek fame and fortune in arms. Of course there was no clear division between the two sorts of knights. A country knight might sometimes go to war, a fighting knight would certainly want to use whatever money he had gained to enlarge his land and improve his castle. The link between knights as a class of landed gentlemen and knights as valiant warriors with high ideals had not vanished.

A knight of about 1340

This brass, in the church of Stoke d'Abernon, Surrey, is to the memory of Sir John d'Abernon who died in 1327. It was a period when knights were experimenting with extra protection against heavy blows and sharp points, and they also seem to have liked to display how well they were clad.

1 Over his shirt and hose the knight would put on, as before, a quilted *aketon* or *gambeson*.

2 Then he would put on his mail *hauberk* and *chausses*.

3 Next, the coat of leather or canvas with iron plates riveted inside – what appear as a decorative design on the outside are probably the beautifully made heads of the rivets. Shaped iron plates were tied or buckled to guard the outer surfaces of arms and legs. It was difficult to cover the inside of joints, but *roundels* were tied to offer some defence at elbow and armpit. Small plates also protect the top of the foot.

Though Sir John is shown with his hands bare as he prays, other pictures show knights at this time with gauntlets of small plates covering the backs of fingers and wrists.

4 Next came the surcoat, and the sword-belt drooping gracefully about the hips – perhaps held by hooks in the fashionable position.

5 Covering the shoulders is another layer of mail, but now it is not part of a coif; it is the *aventail* which is attached to a new style of helmet, the *bascinet*. It seems to have developed because many knights had found the great helm too burdensome for ordinary use. It soon became well shaped to protect most of the head, pointed to deflect blows, and was fitted with a movable visor over the face.

Sir John's shield is painted with the family arms: *azure* (blue), a *chevron or* (gold).

aketon or *gambeson*

hauberk

chausses

coat with iron plates

roundels

gauntlets

surcoat

sword-belt

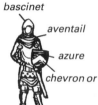
bascinet

aventail

azure

chevron or

8 Reality and romance

Eclipse on the battlefield

English knights had learnt afresh in Scotland, by success at Falkirk in 1298 and disaster at Bannockburn in 1314, some realities of war: that good spearmen on foot could repel armoured horsemen, and that good bowmen could both destroy masses of spearmen and decimate charging cavalry. But if enemy cavalry got amongst them, the bowmen could hardly defend themselves; at this point they needed spearmen to protect them. The English knights were not too proud to get off their horses and take their places as heavily armoured spearmen among the peasant archers, using their knights' lances as spears. For many years this was to prove an unbeatable partnership.

The battle of Crécy

The new tactics achieved their first great victories at Dupplin Moor in 1332, and Halidon Hill in 1333, where large Scottish armies were slaughtered. But in the kingdoms of mainland Europe nobody seems to have recognised that a military revolution had begun on the remote fields of Scotland. It was only in 1346, during the Hundred Years War, when the English did the same thing to a vastly superior army led by the King of France, that the shock reached the knights of Europe.

King Edward III had invaded northern France, achieved very little, and was retreating towards friendly territory in Flanders with the French army close behind. At Crécy he decided to stand and give battle. His plan depended upon the enemy's willingness to attack, but since the French were far more numerous and were eager to catch the invaders there was no doubt about this. The English army was drawn up at the top of a slope. It was in three divisions, two forming the front line and the third, under the king himself, as reserve. Each division had, as its centre, a strong line of armoured

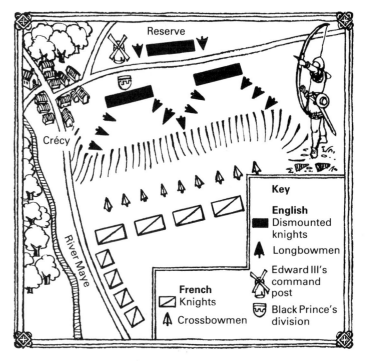

Battle diagram: Crécy, 26 August 1346

knights, squires and men-at-arms, all on foot and acting as spearmen; on each side the archers formed a wing, angled forward towards the enemy. The archers had time to dig many small holes in the ground in front of their position and disguise them with grass, to trip charging horses.

The French nobles and knights were keen to do battle and came upon the English late in the afternoon. They did not wait for their whole army to arrive and form up. They sent forward a line of crossbowmen, experienced mercenaries from Genoa, but as they reached the foot of the slope the first volleys of arrows from the English longbows hissed into them while

From this time onwards full suits of armour have survived, though usually some of their parts originally belonged to different suits. This armour was made in northern Italy, then one of the main centres of the European arms trade.

Now the knight no longer bothers with a surcoat. His limbs are well encased in plate, his coat of plates – velvet-covered here – fits closely, and he follows the new fashion of wearing his sword-belt. The bascinet has developed into what is probably its best-known form, with a jutting visor that allows more air inside the helmet, but has earned the nickname 'pig-faced'.

their own bolts fell short – some say their strings had been slackened by a sudden thunderstorm that had just passed over the battlefield. Falling under the deadly arrows, unable to hit back, the crossbowmen began to recoil. The knights behind them did not let them through. Furious with their 'cowardice' and 'treachery', and eager to get at the English, the French knights tried to ride straight over the crossbowmen. The result was a heaving mass of men and horses at the foot of the slope as the knights struggled to trample and hack their way through the panic-stricken crowd. It was a marvellous target for the English longbowmen.

Eventually some of the French knights got clear and charged up the slope. The nearer they came to the English, the harder the arrows struck. Horses reared and fell, throwing or

trapping knights, and the terrible arrows drove through all but the strongest plates of armour. When they neared the English knights, the French found the arrows criss-crossing as they came between the two wings of archers. They were very brave. They charged again and again, and some actually got to blows with the English knights – this was when the Black Prince 'won his spurs' (see page 47). But the French knights fell in their hundreds and King Edward never needed to use his reserve force.

As they retreated the men who had thought of themselves as the finest knights in the world had to try to cope with the knowledge that all their knightly prowess had been useless against peasants with bows and arrows.

Nobody suggested that knights had suddenly lost their value in war, but some of the French leaders now understood that the old-style charge would never beat the English. In later battles they tried to use their knights in different ways, sometimes in successive waves, sometimes dismounted, but still they never won. After many years, it was only when they accepted the advice of a down-to-earth Breton knight, Bertrand du Guesclin, and refused battle to any English force that had got its archers into position, that the French were able to regain some of their lands by using their superior numbers to cut off and overwhelm English garrisons.

The same pride, confidence in their own strength, greed for honour and glory, and sheer impetuous courage that had made knights so often victorious in the past, now made it very difficult for the French to defeat the English. They now needed caution, well-considered plans, restraint in waiting for the right moment to attack, obedience and discipline. Most of them could not make this mental leap, no matter how often they had to pay the bloody price of remaining fixed in their old attitudes. The most dramatic example of this was not in the war with the English, but far away in Bulgaria, in 1396.

The battle of Nicopolis

During the century since the crusaders had lost their last foothold in the Holy Land, Islam had advanced. The Ottoman Turks now held Asia Minor and had crossed into Europe, taking most of the Balkans. King Sigismund of Hungary raised a great army to drive them back, and called for new crusaders from the West; it was a call that many French nobles and knights felt they could not in honour ignore, and a large number made the long journey to join Sigismund's army.

The Christian and Turkish armies met near Nicopolis. The Turks took up a good position and waited to be attacked. Sigismund decided to send his light horse-archers into the attack first, so as to discover what traps the Turks had prepared. He would keep the French knights, his mighty striking force, until he was sure their charge would have its most shattering effect, and then they would deliver the battle-winning blow. But the French saw this as an insult. It was their right to strike the first blow. Without waiting even for the rest of Sigismund's army to form up, they charged the centre of the Turkish position. They swept aside Turkish light horse-archers, smashed through a thicket of sharpened stakes, broke up Turkish foot-archers and fought more Turkish cavalry to a standstill. It was a magnificent feat of arms – but there was nobody to support them. As they tried to pull themselves together they were struck by a new force of Turkish heavy cavalry, and that was the end. Few of the French knights escaped. The rest of the Christian army then came into action but was eventually routed.

The Turks kept a dozen or so of the most important prisoners for ransom, beheaded several thousand in revenge for a Christian massacre of Turks and enslaved the rest. The French knights' mixture of stupid pride and furious courage was very much what Emperor Leo VI had noted five hundred years earlier (see page 17).

Knights get beaten

It was extremely difficult for a class who had for so long held a privileged position because they were so mighty in battle to accept that their charge was no longer the key to victory. If knights were no longer the masters in war, how long could they remain lords in society?

It was not only the English archers who were destroying the knights' power. In 1302 at Courtrai an army of Flemish peasants and townsmen utterly defeated the French knights who attacked them over marshy ground. They collected 700 pairs of golden spurs from the dead, to hang as thanksgiving in a church. The Flemings used spears and a weapon called a *goedendag*, which may have been a long-handled club with a spear point, but is now thought more likely to have been a sort

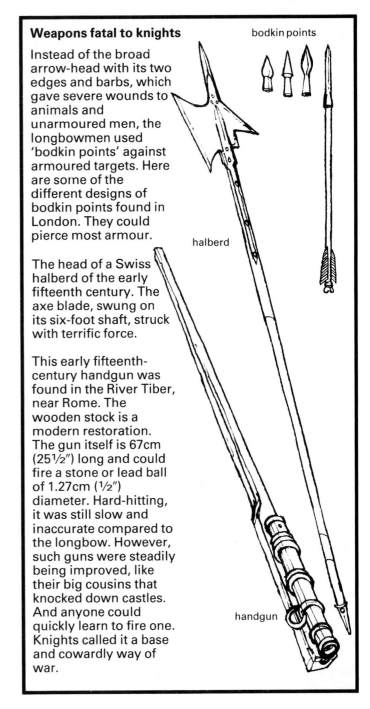

Weapons fatal to knights

bodkin points

Instead of the broad arrow-head with its two edges and barbs, which gave severe wounds to animals and unarmoured men, the longbowmen used 'bodkin points' against armoured targets. Here are some of the different designs of bodkin points found in London. They could pierce most armour.

halberd

The head of a Swiss halberd of the early fifteenth century. The axe blade, swung on its six-foot shaft, struck with terrific force.

This early fifteenth-century handgun was found in the River Tiber, near Rome. The wooden stock is a modern restoration. The gun itself is 67cm (25½") long and could fire a stone or lead ball of 1.27cm (½") diameter. Hard-hitting, it was still slow and inaccurate compared to the longbow. However, such guns were steadily being improved, like their big cousins that knocked down castles. And anyone could quickly learn to fire one. Knights called it a base and cowardly way of war.

handgun

of halberd, with an axe blade. (It got its name from the Flemings' habit of saying 'Good day!' as they struck.) It was certainly the halberd that the Swiss peasants and townsmen used in their battles against the Habsburg dukes of Austria. At Morgarten (1315), Laupen (1339) and Sempach (1386) they overwhelmed the enemy knights, partly by selecting their ground skilfully but mainly by furious fighting. These defeats were shocking; but knights did win later battles with the Flemings, and the Swiss fights could be ignored because they were relatively small and remote and took place in unusual conditions. There was no way, though, of ignoring the English bowmen whose most devastating victory over the French knights came at Agincourt in 1415, under King Henry V.

Yet the English did not win the Hundred Years War. They lost for several reasons: their numbers were small, they made political blunders and the French turned from knights into paid, professional cavalry and took up that most unknightly new weapon, the gun.

The assertion of chivalry

At the very time that knights were losing their centuries-old supremacy in battle, the values of knighthood were being asserted more emphatically then ever, with more elaborate show and ceremonial. This was especially obvious in the many new orders of knighthood that sprang up in almost every kingdom and duchy of western Christendom during the fourteenth and fifteenth centuries.

The old orders and the new

The old crusading orders had lost the Holy Land but were still fighting infidel and heathen. The Templars, however, were destroyed. They did not perish in battle against the Saracens, but at the hands of a Christian king, Philip the Fair of France. In 1307 he listened to accusations that the Templars, corrupted by their pride and riches (see page 26), were no longer serving God, that inside their houses blasphemous rituals and obscene orgies took the place of prayer and the sacraments. The king sent his agents to investigate, and they did their work zealously. By methods that certainly included torture, they got confessions from some Templars, and in 1312 the king persuaded the reluctant Pope to dissolve the entire order, not only in France but everywhere. Their possessions were to be transferred to the Order of St John. It was a cruel and dishonoured end for what had been the greatest of the crusading orders.

The new orders were very different. In the early 1340s Edward III of England was particularly interested in Arthur's knights of the Round Table, and held a great feast and tournament based on that theme in 1344. Four years later he founded a new order of knights – the Order of the Garter. A garter buckled at the knee was to be the badge of his select company of knights. The story is that as he was dancing with the Countess of Salisbury, for whom he was rumoured to feel what may have been courtly love, her garter fell off. The king could guess at the amusement of the watching courtiers, and rebuked them by picking up the blue ribbon and binding it around his own knee. saying 'Honi soit qui mal y pense' (Shame on anyone who thinks ill of it). That became the motto of the new order; so it remains.

As the rules of the order laid down, the members were all to maintain the finest qualities of knighthood, and there is no reason to doubt Edward's sincerity in wanting to encourage and reward chivalry. But he, as we have seen in the way he conducted war, was also a very practical man. He must have seen the advantages of forming around himself a group of the most distinguished knights, bound together by a special loyalty. At a time when the old patterns of feudal obligations in war were being superseded by contracts and pay – he himself was proving a most successful leader in this style – it was well to forge new links with those who could do most to help him. They could be of any rank, from duke to simple knight, but all were equals in chivalry at the meetings of the Order. Also, it soon became useful to try to strengthen friendship with foreign princes and nobles whose alliance was important by inviting them to become members of this small, honoured group of knights.

The Garter was not the first royal order to be founded – in about 1330 the King of Castile created the Knights of the Band, who wore a band or sash of ribbon across the left shoulder – but it seems to have been the one that started a wave of new orders. First came Edward's adversary, King John of France, with his Order of the Star in 1351, then the King of Naples with the Knot in 1352, the Emperor with the Golden Buckle in 1355, and the King of Cyprus with the

the Crescent founded in 1448 by 'Good King' René, Duke of Anjou, a great patron of chivalry who claimed to be King of Naples. Many such orders, like the Star and the Crescent, died with their founders, but others, like the Garter and the Golden Fleece, were inherited by a long line of kings who used them as a way of honouring and rewarding their friends for many generations.

Besides these orders founded by kings, with their mixture of chivalrous and political purposes, there were very many orders set up by noblemen or by groups of knights themselves. Some were mainly to encourage and arrange jousting. The French Marshal Boucicaut founded the Order of the White Lady with the Green Shield, partly to protect women in misfortune and partly to joust with other knights. In Germany there were many associations of knights to arrange tournaments, form teams, enforce rules and check that nobody of low birth or bad behaviour took part.

Germany also had 'brotherhoods' of knights who swore to settle disputes between themselves peacefully by arbitration and to defend one another against all outsiders (except their families or rightful lords). Many of them had reason to seek protection. These were the 'imperial knights' who held their land direct from the emperor as tenants-in-chief (see page 14). Now the emperor's power was fading and the great nobles, prince-bishops and electors, and the rich cities were trying to expand. A knight with a single castle and a village or two needed all the help he could get to remain independent of neighbours like that. These brotherhoods, like the great royal orders of chivalry, had their practical side.

Trying to live up to the code of chivalry

Whenever knight met knight in warfare, they were expected to follow the rules of chivalry. A knight taken prisoner would be treated courteously as a guest. Captives who gave their word not to escape until their ransom was paid were trusted absolutely. Sometimes they even went home to try to raise enough money, and if they failed they returned to their captor until the full sum could be gathered.

War remained cruel, though. The Black Prince humbly waited upon King John of France after capturing him at Poitiers, but before the battle he had been engaged in the usual English strategy of devastating and pillaging great tracts of that same

The Order of the Crescent meets in chapter in 1452. The contemporary illumination shows the knights sitting solemnly, clad alike in the garb of their order, with a statue of their patron, the warrior saint Maurice, dominating their council.

Sword in 1359. So it continued into the next century. One of the most famous was the Golden Fleece of Burgundy founded in 1430; there were also the Swan of Brandenburg, 1444, and

Otterburn, the most chivalrous battle

Jean Froissart, a priest born in about 1338 in Hainault (now in France), wrote the most celebrated chronicle of the earlier half of the Hundred Years War. Though well aware of the cruel side of war, he admired above all the bravery, honour and generosity of true knights. His chronicle was translated into English by Lord Berners in the 1520s, at the request of Henry VIII. Here are some passages from Froissart's account of the battle of Otterburn, 1388, which he regarded as a most chivalrous event, reflecting great honour on all who took part.

[A Scottish army under Earl Douglas was raiding in northern England. In a skirmish outside the walls of Newcastle, Douglas captured the pennon (flag) of the English leader, Sir Henry Percy, known as Hotspur. Douglas marched away but camped at Otterburn, to give Percy a chance to fight to recover the pennon. As soon as he had gathered enough men, Percy marched after him. Night was falling and his men were tired after marching all day, but Hotspur plunged straight into the attack.]

Englishmen on the one party and Scots on the other party are good men of war, for when they meet there is a hard fight without sparing, there is no ho between them as long as spears, swords, axes or daggers will endure, but lay on each upon other, and when they be well beaten, and that the one party hath obtained the victory, they then glorify so in their deeds of arms and are so joyful, that such as be taken they shall be ransomed or they go out of the field, so that shortly each of them is so content with other that at their departing courteously they will say, 'God thank you'; but in fighting one with another there is no play or sparing, and this is true, and that shall well appear by this said rencounter, for it was as valiantly fought as could be devised, as ye shall hear.

Knights and squires were of good courage on both parties to fight valiantly; cowards there had no place, but hardiness reigned with goodly feats of arms, for knights and squires were so joined together at hand strokes, that archers had no place of nother party. There the Scots shewed great hardiness and fought merrily with great desire of honour; the Englishmen were three to one: howbeit, I say not but Englishmen did nobly acquit themselves, for ever the Englishmen had rather been slain or taken in the place than to flee.

[The English began to force the Scots back.]

Then the earl Douglas, who was of great heart and high of enterprise, seeing his men recule back, then to recover the place and to shew knightly valour he took his axe in both his hands, and entered so into the press that he made himself way in such wise, that none durst approach near him, and he was so well armed that he bare well off such strokes as he received. Thus he went forward like a hardy Hector, willing alone to conquer the field and to discomfit his enemies; but at last he was encountered by three spears all at once, the one strake him on the shoulder, the other on the breast and the stroke glinted down to his belly, and the third strake him in the thigh, and sore hurt with all three strokes, so that he was borne perforce to the earth and after that he could not be again relieved. Some of his knights and squires followed him, but not all, for it was night, and no light but by the shining of the moon.

[Few Scots and no English realised that Douglas was dying, and so the confused fight raged on. Hotspur himself was taken prisoner, and at last the exhausted English collapsed.]

This battle was fierce and cruel till it came to the end of the discomfiture; but when the Scots saw the Englishmen recule and yield themselves, then the Scots were courteous and set them to their ransom, and every man said to his prisoner; 'Sir, go and unarm you and take your ease: I am your master'; and so made their prisoners as good cheer as though they had been brothers, without doing to them any damage. . .

Every man may well consider that it was a well fought field, when there were so many slain and taken on both parties.

Knights of about 1480

Armourers in the fifteenth century became so skilful that they could cover a knight almost entirely with plates shaped to fit closely and slide easily. Instead of layer after layer of protection, all the knight needed under his shell was a mail shirt to protect vulnerable gaps like armpits, or a leather suit with patches of mail stitched at these danger points. Now that plates were shaped up to protect the neck and chin, new forms of helmet became popular; the sallet was like a reshaped and deepened kettle hat, and the close helm was hinged to close completely over the head.

The armour for horse and man, the only complete set of its type to have survived, was made in about 1480 in the Bavarian town of Landshut for a member of the Freyberg family, whose castle was not very far away.

The armour on the left was made in about 1450 in Milan. The Milanese style of armour was rounded and smooth to deflect blows, and this fine example has a close helm. The long points on the toes, however, were fashionable rather than practical, and could be discarded for fighting on foot.

king's realm, destroying towns and villages, taking everything and leaving the peasants to starve; and later, at Limoges, which had dared to resist, he let his men massacre the helpless townspeople. Chivalry was between knights. And even they were not spared in time of danger, as when Henry V ordered prisoners to be killed during the battle of Agincourt.

Nevertheless, there were many who believed that war was the noblest occupation, for it called forth all the best qualities of a man, and these were the qualities summed up as knighthood or chivalry. Some men became famous through their whole-hearted efforts to live as perfect knights, such as the French Jean de Boucicaut, the Castilian Pero Niño and the Flemish Jacques de Lalaing. All three partly owe their fame to the way their deeds were described in books written by followers and admirers.

Books were becoming more widespread; increasingly the upper classes were learning to read, and tales of chivalry were popular everywhere. The Flemish chronicler Froissart's account of the first half of the Hundred Years War is full of the exploits of knights. New treatises appeared which explained how to be a good knight; one such book was *Little John of Saintré*, which was written in 1455 by a French squire called Antoine de la Sale. This was a mainly fictional biography, full of sermons about the duties of a knight and descriptions of tournaments and processions. In England, in the 1380s, Chaucer placed a knight whom he obviously admired among the pilgrims of *The Canterbury Tales*, and a century later Caxton printed *Morte d'Arthur*, a book by a knight called Thomas Malory and still the most famous of all the English tales of King Arthur and his knights.

Jousts and tournaments were at least as popular as ever, and often they were lavishly staged. The *pas d'armes* (see page 38) was a form much favoured by those anxious to win fame; for example, in Spain ten knights camped by the bridge of Orbigo from 10 July to 9 August 1434, and jousted with sixty-eight challengers. One spectacle that reflected a fashionable poetic variation on romances of courtly love was the *pas d'armes* of the Shepherdess, which René of Anjou gave at Tarascon in 1449, the year after founding his order of the Crescent. His lady, dressed as a shepherdess and with a flock of real sheep, was defended by two knights, one with a white shield and one with a black, whom other knights were to challenge according to whether they were happy or unhappy in their love.

Jacques de Lalaing,

born in about 1420, came of a distinguished Flemish family, served the Duke of Burgundy, and was reputed to be the most accomplished knight of his time. He toured the courts of western Europe, jousting before the kings. In France he so impressed the ladies that two duchesses gave him favours at the same time and he wore both, a scarf and a glove, on his helmet.

His most famous feat was the *pas d'armes* of the Fountain of Tears, on an island in the river at Chalon-sur-Saône, from 1 November 1449 to 1 October 1450. Here he placed a statue of a lady with a unicorn, both covered with tears and with three shields hanging from the unicorn's neck. At the beginning of each month a herald would attend, and any knight could touch one of the shields to challenge Lalaing to fight with pole-axe, sword or lance. The herald arranged the combats, after making sure that each challenger was of good family. Those who were downed had to pay such forfeits as wearing a gold locked bracelet for a year, or until they found a lady with the key. Lalaing fought more than twenty-two knights here, and at the end he entertained them all to a feast and gave a golden axe, sword and lance to those who had fought best with each weapon.

Lalaing also earned praise in war. In 1453, when Ghent revolted against Burgundy, he had five horses killed under him in one battle as he helped and guided his men in great danger, and was acclaimed the bravest man on the field. A few days later, as he was checking the position of some siege guns, an enemy ball shattered his head. The chief herald of Burgundy, who bore the title of Golden Fleece, wrote an account of his deeds.

Was all this chivalry a response to the lowborn archers, halberdiers and gunners? Was it a pathetic attempt to pretend that nothing had changed, or a proud defiance of the new forces? Men like Edward III may have been fond of chivalry but they were no romantic fools, they were tough realists when it came to politics and war. Perhaps the true meaning of this emphasis on chivalry was that it was an assertion that the nobles and gentlefolk remained above the common crowd, that they alone knew the nature of honour and duty and were fit to lead and rule society.

9 Officers and gentlemen

Soldiers of the king

Knights were a dominant force during the feudal centuries. Their decline came as kings gained a firmer grip, reducing their independent-minded nobles to obedience, and controlling all the armed forces themselves.

The English kings had a system of agreeing contracts with companies of professional soldiers to serve in France (see page 50). After their contracts expired, some became 'free companies' of mercenaries, and if they could not find new employers they lived by robbery and extortion, terrorising parts of war-torn France.

Then King Charles VII issued his ordinance of 1445, creating the *compagnies d'ordonnance*. Each of these companies numbered 100 lances, and each lance consisted of one man-at-arms, two archers and three lightly armed assistants, all mounted: a company of armoured cavalry with supporting troops, in practice. Many of the men were former members of free companies, willing to take the king's pay and help him to make their former comrades leave France. They were regularly paid – a new national tax was imposed specially for this – and in return accepted strict discipline. The men-at-arms were equipped exactly as knights, and many were in fact knights or even nobles who preferred this to being with companies of robbers. The *compagnies d'ordonnance* were the first regular standing army in Europe, and, since they still looked and fought like knights, the knights in its ranks seem to have slipped easily into their new role.

All over Europe, as the power and prestige of the kings increased, it became most honourable and profitable to serve them. Several royal armies came to include cavalry regiments, usually part of the Household troops, where every soldier had to be a nobleman or gentleman. Meanwhile, though, cavalry ceased to be seen as the main strength of armies. In the sixteenth century Spain was the foremost military power, and the

In the great wars between Renaissance monarchs, battlefields still shook sometimes under the charge of armoured horsemen.

This is how the German artist Hans Burgkmair visualised the victory of his master, Emperor Maximilian, and the English King Henry VIII over the French at Thérouanne in 1513. The French cavalry (successors of the compagnies d'ordonnance) *unexpectedly met the main Anglo-Imperial force, and tried to get away. Their retreat became a chase that the English gleefully called the Battle of the Spurs. The French knights of earlier centuries would never have obeyed their general's order to retreat.*

A knight of about 1590

By this time few soldiers wore full armour. It was more common to use only half or three-quarter armour, protecting head, chest, shoulders and perhaps arms and thighs.

Meanwhile armourers had lost none of their skill. For wealthy men they produced strong and richly decorated suits, which would look impressive in processions and parades. With them they supplied extra pieces, some to reinforce the armour for jousting, some as alternatives – open helmets, for instance – in case the owner wished to be more lightly equipped.

The photograph shows an armour with parts of two such sets, one belonging to Sir John Smythe, a very experienced soldier who believed armour was still useful in war and argued that the longbow was a better weapon than the musket – in which he was right, but the musket required far less training.

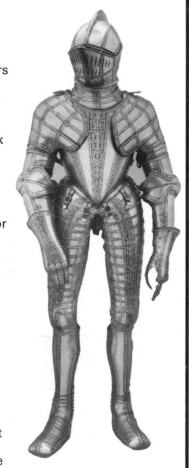

pride of her army were the pikemen. Gentlemen then thought it no dishonour to enlist in a *tercio* and, in Shakespeare's phrase, 'trail the puissant pike'. (Being a musketeer was less honourable, since it did not demand the courage and strength of hand-to-hand fighting.)

As regular armies developed, regular officers were needed. Naturally these would come from the classes that had always led in war, the nobility and gentry. As the pattern of ranks in the military hierarchy became recognised and respected, they could take pride in a set of new titles such as Captain, Colonel or General. The gentry who had formerly been the knightly class became the officer class.

The transformation into royal officers seems to have been gradual and smooth in most kingdoms. The country where trouble erupted was where there was no strong national monarch and where a class of knights had long felt under threat from their more powerful neighbours.

The Knights' War in Germany

In the early sixteenth century the imperial knights of Germany were in a worse position than ever, because financial inflation was making them poorer, and they were unable to live on the rents from their lands. Some became mercenary captains and others became robbers, forcing merchants and peasants to pay tolls and tributes. It was a time when Germany was in ferment with new ideas and questions, the time of the Renaissance. Writers and preachers were exposing and ridiculing the mistakes, follies and corruptions of those who claimed to be in authority – especially churchmen.

As the mood of discontent grew stronger, a group of knights led by Franz von Sickingen thought the time was ripe to act. In 1522 they proclaimed that the Church was rotten and that its vast wealth ought to be seized and put to better use. Then they attacked Trier, the city of one of Germany's wealthiest archbishops. They hoped that townsmen and peasants would rise to help them, but the common people had seen too much pride and greed among the knights themselves. The city of Trier held out, the neighbouring princes gathered an army and the Knights' War collapsed. Henceforward the German knights had no choice but to enter the service of princes, like the knights in other countries.

The last of the knights

Royal power extended over the crusading orders too. Prince Henry the Navigator began the great age of European exploration and founded the Portuguese overseas empire with men and ships of the Order of Christ, which he happened to be administering. In Spain the king had himself elected head of all the orders, and got the Pope to confirm this and make it permanent.

Only the knights of St John remained an independent fighting order. Driven from Rhodes by the Turks in 1522 after an epic siege, they established themselves in Malta. Again the Turks attacked, in 1565, and there was an even more heroic struggle against terrible odds. This time the knights won. It was the last and greatest victory of the crusading orders. The knights remained in Malta for another two centuries, but the Holy War gradually degenerated into little better than pirate raids on both sides.

The sixteenth century saw the end of knights in war. By the end of the century the only fully armoured cavalry likely to be seen on a western European battlefield would be wearing black bullet-resistant plates and firing pistols at one another. Splendid armour was still being constructed, but not for war; it was to make princes and their friends look magnificent in parades. By 1600 even this fashion was waning.

Don Quixote

Knights belonged to the past. Yet it sometimes seemed that the myth of knighthood was replacing the reality. In Spain particularly there was an insatiable appetite for tales of knights who routed hordes of Infidels, slew dreadful monsters and overcame the enchantments of wicked magicians; and, of course, were amply rewarded by their ladies and their kings. It was reading book after book of this nonsense, wrote Miguel de Cervantes, that turned the mind of Don Quixote.

In Cervantes' classic story, set in Spain in about 1600, Don Quixote rides off to be a knight-errant in the real world. Deluded by the romances he had read, he imagined inns to be castles, windmills to be giants, and the brass bowl of a barber to be a legendary helmet. As we watch Don Quixote going from one comic misadventure to another, we could easily think that Cervantes is poking fun mercilessly at the whole idea of knighthood. In fact he is doing the opposite; he is trying to strip away the silly tales of marvels that were hiding what was true and good. Absurd and foolish as he may seem, Don Quixote is never anything but brave and honest, trying to protect and rescue the oppressed, and sometimes speaking with such wisdom and kindness as to shame those who would mock him. Perhaps it is folly to ride forth in armour as if this were the world of King Arthur, and not to understand the realities of life, but, writes Cervantes, the essential knightly

In the nineteenth century the French artist Gustave Doré produced a famous set of illustrations of Don Quixote. *This is how it all begins, with the knight reading romances of chivalry and imagining himself the hero of fantastic adventures.*

qualities of loyalty, honesty, generosity and courtesy, which are summed up in the word chivalry, still remain true.

Distant echoes

The medieval knights left much behind. Their descendants, the gentry, continued as rulers of the countryside. Many of them in England had no wish to be knighted and remained squires, but they were so powerful a class by the eighteenth century that some historians have called them the 'Squire-archy'.

Other people did value titles. and were ready to pay to be addressed as 'Sir'. James I was able to raise money by inventing and selling the new title of baronet, which was hereditary and superior to the rank of knight. The old orders of knighthood remained useful for rewarding the king's – or government's – friends. England still had the Order of the Garter, but its numbers were limited. To increase them would reduce the value of the order. Instead, it seemed better to revive former orders and create new ones: for England, the Bath, created in 1725; for Scotland, the Thistle, in 1687; for Ireland, St Patrick, in 1783. All the states of Europe were using this cheap and easy method of recognising good service.

These survivals were merely the trappings of knighthood. Did nothing survive of its spirit? The conduct expected of an 'officer and a gentleman' in a modern army shows strong similarities to the code of chivalry. But the ideals of chivalry may have spread much more widely.

After centuries of disfavour, things medieval were brought into fashion by the Romantic Revival of the nineteenth century. The admiration went deeper than a liking for Gothic architecture and the novels of Walter Scott. Religious leaders looked back to the Christian inspiration of the Middle Ages, and in the fast-growing public schools of Victorian England no effort was spared to turn middle-class boys into Christian gentlemen. Tennyson wrote *The Idylls of the King* about Arthur and his knights, and made the best of them declare, 'My strength is as the strength of ten because my heart is pure.' After Conan Doyle wrote of *Sir Nigel* and *The White Company* some critics said his hero was more like a Victorian gentleman than a medieval knight. Perhaps the two had more in common than the critics allowed.

Albrecht Dürer of Nuremberg lived from 1471 to 1528, a time when knights were making their last efforts to survive as a real force in a changing world.

In 1513 he engraved The Knight, *but it is usually known as* The Knight, Death and the Devil. *As with some of his other pictures, Dürer has left it to us to find the meaning for ourselves. Resolutely the knight rides on, unworried by the warning of Death and a grotesque little Devil. This may be how a great artist saw the knights, after their centuries of leadership, riding into history.*